HEROES OF HISTORY

MILTON HERSHEY

More Than Chocolate

HEROES OF HISTORY

MILTON HERSHEY

More Than Chocolate

JANET & GEOFF BENGE

P.O. BOX 635, LYNNWOOD, WA 98046

Emerald Books are distributed through YWAM Publishing. For a full
list of titles, including other great biographies, visit our website at
www.ywampublishing.com or call 1-800-922-2143.

Milton Hershey: More Than Chocolate
Copyright © 2012 by Janet and Geoff Benge

Published by Emerald Books
P.O. Box 635
Lynnwood, Washington 98046

This title is available as an e-book. Visit www.ywampublishing.com.

Library of Congress Cataloging-in-Publication Data
Benge, Janet, 1958–
Milton Hershey : more than chocolate / Janet and Geoff Benge.
    p. cm. — (Heroes of history)
  Includes bibliographical references.
  ISBN 978-1-932096-82-8 (pbk.)
  1. Hershey, Milton Snavely, 1857–1945—Juvenile literature. 2.
Businesspeople—United States—Biography—Juvenile literature.
3. Hershey Foods Corporation—History—Juvenile literature. 4.
Chocolate industry—United States—History—Juvenile literature. I.
Benge, Geoff, 1954- II. Title.
  HD9200.U52H463 2012
  338.7'66392092—dc23
  [B]   2012031689

First printing 2012

Printed in the United States of America

HEROES OF HISTORY
Biographies

Abraham Lincoln
Alan Shepard
Benjamin Franklin
Christopher Columbus
Clara Barton
Davy Crockett
Daniel Boone
Douglas MacArthur
George Washington
George Washington Carver
Harriet Tubman
John Adams
John Smith
Laura Ingalls Wilder
Meriwether Lewis
Milton Hershey
Orville Wright
Ronald Reagan
Theodore Roosevelt
Thomas Edison
William Penn

More Heroes of History coming soon!
Unit study curriculum guides are available
for select biographies.

Available at your local bookstore or
through Emerald Books
1 (800) 922-2143

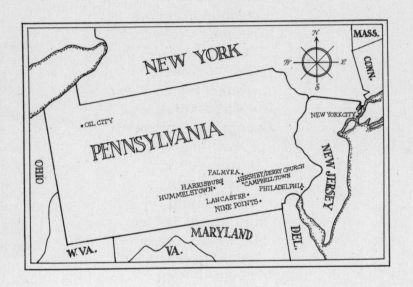

Contents

Chapter 1

Failure

M ilton Hershey stared gloomily out the window of the train as New Jersey gave way to Pennsylvania. He should have been glad to be heading home, but he was anything but. The huffing of the steam locomotive and the constant thumping of the steel wheels on the rails seemed to compound the gloom he was feeling. He had failed in business yet again. His first failure was a bruising experience, but the second had been crushing. He was supposed to have learned things the first time around that would help him avoid a second failure, but it had not worked out that way.

Now Milton was riding the train back to Lancaster, Pennsylvania. He hadn't even had enough money to pay to ship his equipment home. Instead, his aunt had sent it freight forward for him, and

Milton would have to pay the stationmaster in Lancaster before he could get it back. He supposed he might never be able to redeem the equipment.

It wasn't that Milton had not worked hard. He had—sometimes going without sleep for days on end. But no matter how hard he worked, it never seemed to be sufficient. At the end of each month, there was not enough money coming in to match the business's monthly outgoings. Milton slowly sank deeper and deeper into a financial hole until he could no longer keep up with the rent or pay for the raw materials he needed.

At first Milton's mother's family had helped him financially, and Milton had been glad for their support. But with this second failure, the family's faith in him and their support had been withdrawn. Milton wasn't even sure whether any of his relatives would want to see him when he got back home.

Milton had started with such high hopes and had ended with so little. Even he had to admit he seemed to be following his father's path. Henry Hershey had always had great dreams for the future and the fortunes he would make, but his dreams never came to anything—like the time he moved his young family to the oil fields of western Pennsylvania, determined to strike it rich.

Chapter 2

Derry Church

It was January 1862, and four-year-old Milton Hershey peered out the window of the shanty at the fresh coat of white powder. He marveled at how pretty Oil City, Pennsylvania, looked draped in snow. His mother, Fanny, continually told him not to get the oil-slick mud from the settlement's narrow roads on his clothes, but that was an impossible task. A layer of oil seemed to cover every surface in town, including a slick on the nearby Allegheny River. But now the town was all submerged beneath crisp whiteness. Sometimes Milton's mother sat him on her knee and told him of a different place 250 miles away, with green grass, powder-blue sky, and cows grazing lazily in the meadows. Milton knew she was talking about the place they had lived before his father, Henry Hershey, had gotten a harebrained idea, as his mother put it. Henry had moved the small family in September 1860 from Derry Church, Pennsylvania, northwest to Oil City to make a fortune in America's first oil boom.

Even though Milton was only four years old, he was aware of the differences between his parents. His mother worked hard, cooking over a tiny gas flame and saving her pennies in a pocket under her apron. She tried to keep the shanty clean and stuffed old rags into cracks in the wall to keep out the cold. His father, on the other hand, was always laughing and telling stories. He didn't seem to know where the next penny was coming from, and it seemed that he hardly cared. Sometimes Henry would come home from a day of "work," not with the money to buy potatoes and corn but with a book he had accepted as payment for his labor. When this happened, Milton braced himself. He knew it would lead to an argument between his parents. His mother did not like his father reading books. She liked to see men working hard—plowing, planting, weeding, harvesting—all the activities her brothers and father carried out on a well-run Mennonite farm.

As Milton stared out the shanty window, he saw two men walking briskly through the fresh snow. Somehow they looked out of place. "Look, Mama," he said.

Fanny glanced out the window and gasped. "Milton, don't say a word," she said, straightening her plain gray skirt and adjusting her bonnet.

Milton watched as the two men stopped outside the shanty door and knocked. His mother's hands trembled as she pulled up the crossbar on the latch and swung the door open. The strangers stared at her. "Fanny?" the taller one said.

"Of course it's me," she said briskly. "Why have you come?"

The taller man stepped into the room, quickly surveying the single chair and table made from a discarded barrel. He looked at Milton's mother carefully. "So this it what it's come to, has it? And another baby on the way, I take it?"

Milton's mother nodded. "Due in spring," she replied, turning toward her son. "Milton, these are your uncles, Abraham and Benjamin. Say good day to them."

Milton stammered for words. He was shy, and he couldn't remember meeting a relative before. "Hello," he finally said.

"Now go and fetch your father. I think he's at Mr. Hughes's house. If not, ask where he is and tell him my brothers are here to see us."

Milton did not need to put on a coat. He was already wearing every piece of warm clothing he owned. He headed through the blinding white snow toward the Hugheses' place. Milton knew that his father loved to spend time there, spinning yarns and talking with Mr. Hughes about the possibilities of oil and what they would do when they struck it rich.

Sure enough, Milton found his father talking and laughing with Mr. Hughes and several other men. Henry stopped laughing when he heard that Uncle Benjamin and Uncle Abraham were waiting for him at their shanty. "Darn interfering lot!" he muttered under his breath as he stepped outside. "What do they want now?"

Milton did not know what his uncles wanted, but he had the feeling he was about to find out. When he and his father got back to the shanty, the two men were busy stuffing the family's pots and plates into a pillowcase.

"We're taking Fanny and the boy back with us, Henry," Uncle Benjamin said. "It's up to you if you come or not, but our sister's not staying here one more day. This place is an abomination."

Milton wasn't sure what *abomination* meant, but he knew it wasn't a good thing.

Henry sighed deeply. "But I'm so close!" he said, his eyes shining. "If you come with me, I'll show you an oil derrick that's just netted a man I know over thirty thousand dollars. He was a teamster who took an 8 percent share in a well in return for hauling in the lumber and machinery to sink the well. It struck oil and he was rich overnight. I have shares in a claim near the creek, and I know it's going to be a gusher soon. Do you know how much oil there is under this ground? It's like money just waiting to be drilled up."

Uncle Benjamin shook his head, his face steely. "Enough of your stories, Henry. The empty potato box tells the tale plain enough. Fanny's agreed to come with us, and the boy needs a steady home and some good food. He's as skinny as a rake. Are you coming with us or not?"

Milton watched as his father's shoulders slumped forward. "What choice are you giving me?" Henry said.

"Whatever choice you want," Uncle Abraham replied. "But make your decision fast. We're not spending a moment longer in this Sodom and Gomorrah than we have to."

"It's a mistake, I tell you, a huge mistake," Henry persisted. "You have to take risks to get ahead these days."

By now Milton's two uncles had gathered up everything in the hut except for the furniture. "There's a wagon waiting down the street. If you're not there when we're done loading this into it, we'll leave without you," Abraham said.

Milton's father picked up his pile of books, tied them into a bundle with string, and walked out the door behind the uncles.

Uncle Abraham guided the horse and wagon through Oil City to the banks of the Allegheny River. The meager cargo of Hershey-family belongings was transferred to a small riverboat, and once everything and everyone was aboard, the vessel set out down the river. Several miles downstream the family arrived at the town of Franklin, where the group transferred to a paddle steamer. Milton had never seen such a large boat and was entranced by the large paddle wheel at the back of the steamer. The paddle wheel seemed to force the vessel forward by thrashing the water. The steamboat had more than one deck, and Milton loved the sweeping downriver view from the top. As he took in the sights, though, soot settled on his head and arms from the steamer's two large funnels. Milton decided he preferred to have snow rather than soot falling from the sky.

Eventually the group reached Pittsburgh, a city of about fifty thousand residents, with houses set in neat rows and large factories that lined the river, emitting smoke and coal dust into the air. Milton had never experienced a settlement as big as Pittsburgh. People seemed to be hustling and bustling everywhere. In Pittsburgh the family transferred from the paddle steamer to a train for the trip back east across Pennsylvania. As the steam locomotive hauled the train, Milton sat with his nose to the window, watching farms and towns and forest roll by. And as the train rolled along, he realized he was traveling faster than he'd ever thought possible.

The journey fascinated Milton, and it ended in the tiny town of Derry Church in southeast Pennsylvania. Before he had time to think about it, Milton was embraced by so many relatives he began to imagine that everyone he met in the town was related to him, and they probably were. Swiss families who had come to North America seeking religious freedom in the 1700s had settled Derry Church and the surrounding farmland. These settlers called themselves Mennonites, a Christian group who followed the teaching formalized in the sixteenth century by a man named Menno Simons. The Snavelys, Milton's mother's family, and the Hersheys traced their roots back to these early settlers. And while the Snavelys were still devout Mennonites and Milton's grandfather Snavely was a bishop in the Reformed Mennonite Church, Milton's father, Henry, had strayed from the strict rules of the group.

Milton loved his new life in Derry Church. His parents moved into the old stone farmhouse on the Hershey farm where Milton and his father had been born. It was still winter, and Milton enjoyed warming himself by the crackling fire that burned in the huge stone fireplace. He loved watching the flames devour the logs. Although it was too early to plant crops, there were plenty of other farm chores Milton could do. He learned how to collect eggs from the henhouse, fetch water from the kitchen well, and feed scraps to the chickens. He also spent hours listening to his older cousins tell stories about swimming in the creek in the summer, eating watermelon, and catching fish in the pond. Milton could hardly wait for the spring thaw, which arrived on April 12, 1862, a day when something wonderful happened. His mother gave birth to a beautiful, black-haired daughter. Henry and Fanny named her Sarena, and Milton enjoyed helping take care of his new sister.

The arrival of spring meant it was time to plant crops. The fields had to be prepared and plowed, and then seeds were planted along neat furrows. Milton loved the landscape around Derry Church— the rolling green hills, the neatly plowed fields, the blossoming apple trees. After the mud and petroleum slicks of Oil City, he decided it must be the prettiest place in the world.

Summer and fall were even more exciting for Milton, as he was often allowed to go to the nearby city of Harrisburg, where the Hershey family sold the produce they had harvested, along with the butter and cheese they had produced on the farm. Milton would help his mother at the small rented booth at the market, watching as she carefully stored away the coins she received as payment for the produce. Milton's father would stand at the side of the booth and talk with local townspeople about the latest book or magazine article he had read or about politics. Sometimes when his mother was busy selling and his father was deep in conversation, Milton would sneak away to explore the streets of Harrisburg.

One of the topics that always seemed to come up in Henry Hershey's conversations in Harrisburg was the civil war being fought between the northern and southern states. Milton's father was always eager to catch up on news of various battles. To Milton, the war seemed to have been going on for as long as he could remember, with talk of a string of bloody battles—Bull Run, Shiloh, Antietam, and Fredericksburg. Even though his father had tried to explain it to Milton, it was hard for Milton to grasp the idea of war. After all, the war was being fought in faraway places, not in Pennsylvania, and since his family were Mennonites who refused to bear arms, they were not called up to fight. However, in June 1863, when Milton was five years old, all that changed.

Talk among the local community began to focus on the possibility of the war coming to Derry Church. People said General Robert E. Lee and his Confederate army were marching toward Pennsylvania with the intention of invading the state. On June 28 news reached Derry Church that the town of York, Pennsylvania, located just twenty-five miles south down the Lebanon Valley, had surrendered to the Confederates without a shot being fired. Milton hoped his father would be able to protect him and his baby sister Sarena if Confederate soldiers arrived at Derry Church.

Milton thought of his own hoard—the four pennies he had saved. He had something to protect. If the Confederates invaded the local community, the coins had to be kept safe. After dinner one night, Milton took a hand trowel from the barn and walked to the middle of the cornfield, where he dug a hole. He took careful note of the exact location of the hole before he placed his precious coins into a coffee can and buried them. Patting the soil down over the can, he was satisfied no one would find them.

On July 1 Milton awoke to a strange sound, one he had never heard before. It was a low, rumbling sound, similar to thunder, but was coming out of a clear blue sky. Milton got out of bed and ran to the kitchen, where his mother was cooking oatmeal. His father was standing by the open door, looking out.

"What's that sound, Mama?" Milton asked.

"Cannons," his father replied, "cannon fire from the south. A mighty battle is raging this morning."

Within an hour Milton began to see Conestoga covered wagons rumbling northward filled with neighbors fleeing the area. The Hersheys, however, chose to stay where they were. Milton braced himself for the worst, rehearsing what he would do if Confederate soldiers overran the farm and attacked the family.

As it turned out, Milton's bravery was not tested. The cannon fire he heard marked the beginning of battle in a different town, Gettysburg. The Battle of Gettysburg raged on for three days as Major General George Meade and his Union Army of the Potomac clashed with Robert E. Lee's Confederate forces. Lee was defeated in the battle, and his forces retreated, ending the attempted invasion of Pennsylvania.

With the invasion threat over, the Conestoga wagons returned and things got back to normal. Henry assured Milton that the war would end soon, telling him the South was weak and couldn't hold out much longer against the North.

Now that the Confederate army had been beaten back, Milton decided it was safe to dig up his can of pennies. There was just one problem: the corn in the cornfield had grown in the intervening days, confusing Milton as to where exactly he had buried the can. He dug numerous holes in search of his pennies, but no matter how hard he tried, he could not find the spot. Milton felt miserable. When he told his father about the situation, Henry laughed and told Milton that he may have been the only person in all Lancaster County who lost everything he owned in the War Between the States.

By fall of 1863 Henry decided it was time for Milton to go to school. Like so many other things in Milton's life, this caused an argument between his parents. Fanny did not like the idea of sending a five-year-old off to school. She wanted Milton to grow up to be a good Mennonite farmer, raising crops, marrying, and being a respectable man in the community. This, she pointed out, could all be accomplished with a minimal amount of schooling. Henry wanted Milton's education to begin as soon as possible. He had ideas of Milton becoming a famous writer, something he himself would have loved to have become if he'd had a better education. Sometimes Milton held his hands over his ears as he lay in bed listening to his parents argue about school. The bickering made him feel miserable, but not as miserable as the thought of actually sitting at a desk all day long.

Chapter 3

School

M ilton walked slowly through the eastern hemlock grove toward the Derry Church schoolhouse. There was no way to avoid going, and he dreaded what lay ahead. Sitting at a desk all day long seemed like torture, and to make matters worse, his father's younger brother Elias was the schoolmaster. Milton knew he was not going to get away with misbehaving or not paying attention. He would have to concentrate and work hard or Uncle Elias would surely tell his father.

Discouraged, Milton arrived at school and sat down in the front row with the other six-year-old boys and girls starting school in the fall of 1863. Milton had just turned six several days before on September 13. All of the other children were bigger than he was, and one girl could already recite the alphabet. Milton frowned; he felt he was already behind the others.

As the weeks passed, Milton struggled to keep up with his lessons. No matter what he did, he found it nearly impossible to distinguish the letters of the alphabet from each other, especially the capitals and their lowercase forms. Why, he asked himself, didn't a capital *A* and a lowercase *a* look the same? Not to mention the capital and lowercase *Q* or *R*. He hated staring at the jumble of letters on the page, trying to decide what a letter's name was and what it sounded like. Eventually he was able to read simple words, but a sentence about a cat sitting on a mat or the rain on the plain bored him. Where was the adventure in that?

As he looked around the schoolroom, Milton concluded that he was not the only one asking that question. Many of the boys in class were restless, pushing and pinching each other when Uncle Elias was not watching. In fact, the main amusement of the day was "scrouging," where boys seated in the middle of a bench would push hard against the others until the boy at the end of the bench fell off. Apart from watching the fuss Uncle Elias made trying to figure out who had caused the disruption, Milton's favorite pastime at school was fetching drinking water in a bucket from the stream. He loved being outside, listening to the birds and soaking up the winter sun.

Every night Milton's father quizzed him about what he had learned at school that day. Henry was more interested in world events than most men raised Mennonite, and it was clear to Milton that his father wanted him to have good general knowledge. But most nights Milton could not answer the questions his father posed, and he began to wonder whether he would ever remember the names of the countries of the world and which states were fighting for the North and the South in the War Between the States. Other countries, even other states, all seemed so far away from rural Pennsylvania.

School ended with the arrival of spring, when students were all needed back on their family farms to help with the planting and tending of crops. Milton was no exception. His father spent hours at a time dreaming up get-rich-quick schemes, leaving Milton and his mother to do the work. Even so, there was barely enough money to keep the family from starving. Milton sold wild blackberries and home-made corn brooms door-to-door around the area, trying to make a few extra pennies for his mother and sister.

The arrival of fall 1864 signaled the start of another school year. This time Milton's parents sent him to a school in nearby Rockledge. It was farther away—a three-mile walk each way—but they hoped the new schoolteacher would have better control over the students than Uncle Elias had. This made little difference to Milton. He was just as miserable with Mr. Moyer at the new school as he had been with his uncle at the previous one. The letters of the alphabet still refused to form themselves easily into words that he could read. Milton began to wonder whether he would ever learn to read properly and what point there was in doing so.

The most exciting event of that school year, according to the adults, was the end of the War Between the States on April 9, 1865. Except for his lost pennies, the war had hardly impacted Milton in Pennsylvania. But the rest of the community was relieved that the fighting had come to an end. And even though Mennonites took little interest in politics, the whole community was saddened when news arrived that five days after the end of the war, President Abraham Lincoln had been shot and killed while attending a performance at Ford's Theatre in Washington, DC. On April 22, 1865, the train carrying the body of President Lincoln back to Springfield, Illinois, for burial passed through nearby Lancaster.

In September 1865, soon after Milton's eighth birthday, Henry Hershey announced that the family was moving, not across the state this time, but forty miles south to Nine Points, where he had leased a forty-four-acre farm. Milton was swept away with the excitement in his father's eyes as he talked about the new place. "Son, you mark my words, this farm is going to be unlike anything anyone around here has ever seen. It's going to be an experimental farm. I've read about them in books—Thomas Jefferson had one. We're going to grow new species of trees and grass, and better yet, we are going to farm something I bet you've never thought could be farmed."

His father stopped, and Milton waited for him to continue.

"Go on, boy. Guess."

Milton hardly knew what to say, but his father expected an answer. "We could farm oranges,"

Milton said, thinking of the most exotic fruit he had ever seen.

His father laughed. "No, too cold here. The snow would nip them. Something much better than that—fish!"

Milton frowned. He had no idea how his father intended to farm fish, but he knew he was going to find out.

The following week the four members of the Hershey family moved to Nine Points. Henry sang and waved to people while his wife sat quietly as they rode along. Sarena giggled at her father, and Milton didn't know what to think. His original enthusiasm had been dampened by his mother's dismissive comments about the move.

Soon the wagon passed through the gates of the new farm. "The first thing I am going to do is have a sign made," Milton's father said with enthusiasm. "The Trout Brook Fruit and Nursery Farm. What do you think of that for a name, boy?" he said, tousling Milton's brown hair.

Milton smiled back at his father, hoping that this scheme would go well.

At first, things looked promising. The local Mennonite community showed up at the Hershey's farm to see how they could help. It was their way of welcoming a new neighbor. They brought tools with them and expected to be put to work. Henry had plenty for them to do. His idea was to build a seven-foot-high dam on the creek and stock it with trout, which could be caught and sold. Henry also planted rows and rows of small specimen fruit trees that he had mail-ordered from the coast, hoping to sell them to city folk in Lancaster and Harrisburg when the trees got bigger. Over time, Henry also experimented with growing roses and berries and breeding uncommon cattle and poultry. He even sent away to Minnesota for alfalfa seeds. No one in Pennsylvania had seen alfalfa plants, but Henry had read about them and was convinced they would make good cattle feed.

As he had done with his other endeavors, Milton's father started with great enthusiasm. But before long Milton was doing more of the actual labor while his father thought up new schemes. The Trout Brook Fruit and Nursery Farm was within walking distance of McComsey's hotel and general store, where Henry spent more and more of his time. He loved meeting travelers and hearing about what was happening in the rest of the country. He learned that oil was now up to twelve dollars a barrel, and he blamed his wife and her brothers for making him leave Oil City. If they had stayed, surely a fortune would have been his.

Soon Henry had his eyes on another potential goldmine. It came in the form of plans for a machine—a perpetual-motion machine. One of Henry's new tavern friends was an eccentric German immigrant named Conrad Wohlgast. Conrad convinced Henry that he was on the verge of creating the world's first perpetual-motion machine, which could keep running forever without any outside source of energy. Milton tried to be enthusiastic as his father showed him the diagrams of rods and weights that spun around a wheel, but he had a sinking feeling. The more wrapped up his father became in this new venture, the more work Milton would have to do on the farm.

Milton's new school in Nine Points started out in a one-room school above a chicken house, but the teacher soon became discouraged and closed it. From there Milton attended another school called Old Harmony, but he did not stay long. A neighbor had offered to pay Milton an allowance to walk his five-year-old daughter to a school that was in the opposite direction of Milton's. Milton was interested in earning money, so once again he changed schools.

Milton looked forward to the day when Sarena would be able to walk to school with him and his young charge. However, this was not to be. In early spring of 1867, just before her fifth birthday, Sarena came down with scarlet fever, the most common childhood illness that killed young children. The whole Hershey family prayed that Sarena would be spared. Fanny sat beside her daughter day and night. She spooned willow bark tea down Sarena's swollen throat and massaged her arms and legs. But her best efforts did not help. On March 31, 1867, Sarena died.

Milton was too stunned to say much as he watched Sarena's body being placed in a pine coffin and lowered into the grave his uncles had dug for her. His little sister was gone, just when she was nearly old enough to have adventures with. Milton knew he would always have a dull spot in his heart when he thought of her.

Just as bad as losing Sarena was the extra attention Milton now received from both of his parents. He felt like a worm caught between two birds, each pulling him in the opposite direction. The situation eased somewhat when his mother's sister, Aunt Mattie, came to live with the family to help them recover from Sarena's death. Aunt Mattie seemed to dislike Milton's father intensely, and she sided with his mother on every issue. She was soon Milton's staunchest ally, urging him to try his best at school.

Milton tried to focus on his studies, but he had changed schools so many times he was hopelessly behind and was sure he would never catch up. He knew he would not be the writer his father wanted him to be, and he had no interest in becoming a farmer. There had to be something else, something that he was really suited for. But what?

The situation came to a head in 1870 when Milton was twelve. He had been sent to yet another school. The teacher, Thomas Good, visited the Hershey family. It was not a pleasant meeting. Mr. Good kindly pointed out that Milton might not be ready for the advanced subject matter he taught at Valley Academy. Milton's father would hear none of it. In his view Milton had a brilliant mind that needed a good teacher to draw it out. Much to Milton's embarrassment, Mr. Good and his father soon entered into a shouting match. Even more horrifying, Henry challenged Milton's teacher to a fight. Milton fled the scene and did not return until after the teacher had left.

Things were a little calmer when Milton entered the house again. He was embarrassed by his father's behavior, and even more embarrassed that his poor grades were the cause of the fight. Milton knew one thing for sure: he could not go back to Valley Academy. It was time for another change.

Thankfully, Fanny appeared to feel the same way. "Can't you see the boy has had enough of schooling?" she snapped at her husband. "It would be much better to find someone to take him on as an apprentice. He could learn a trade and start to make his own way in the world."

Milton looked expectantly at his father. Would he agree? Was he really finished with the humiliation of being constantly behind at school?

Henry smiled. Milton took it as a good sign. "Perhaps you're right," he said. "Why, just this morning I was talking to someone who is in need of an apprentice. Yes, indeed, I think this could work out well after all. I will speak to the man about the matter in the morning."

Milton wanted to ask for more details, but he knew from his father's tone of voice that there would be no more said until tomorrow.

That night Milton took stock of his life. He was twelve and a half years old, small for his age. He had a high voice like a girl, and Mr. Good had told his father he had a fourth-grade education. He wondered what his father was about to sign him up for. Apprentices were boys and young men who learned a trade from an experienced master tradesman. The trade could be anything from shoemaking to tailoring to wheelwrighting or clock making. The question was, whom had his father been talking to? What kind of plan had he hatched that would make him willing to let Milton leave school for good? Milton was sure there must be some positive answers to the question, but his stomach turned all night—especially when he recalled that an apprentice normally lived on his master's premises. Could this be his last night at home?

Chapter 4

"Tell Your Father You Are Useless!"

Henry burst through the door, a blast of cold air rushing into the kitchen behind him. Milton looked up from the bowl of soup he was eating and saw a glint in his father's eye as he quickly closed the door. "Well," he said, walking over to Milton, "Sam Ernst says he'll have you, and I've put down a deposit. What do you think of that, boy? A printer! Sam will make a printer out of you."

Milton's heart sank. Yesterday he was glad to be done with books and school, and today his father had signed him over to be a printer's apprentice. Now he would never be done with books.

Milton's father hardly seemed to notice his son's silence or lack of enthusiasm. "Just think of it, you'll be the first person to read the newspaper each week. You will have to be sure to keep me informed of the

33

latest scientific breakthroughs. I'll be relying on you," he chuckled.

This time Milton tried to smile, but he could hardly believe his father had signed him up to learn how to print the newspaper. Milton had seen Sam Ernst at the general store. Mr. Ernst was a short, stocky man, unsmiling and uncompromising in his plain black clothes and broad-brimmed hat. Of all the trades Milton had imagined during the night, he had never even considered being a printer's apprentice.

By the following morning Milton was living with Sam Ernst at Pequea Creek. It was only five miles north of Nine Points, though it felt like a thousand miles away. The task ahead, even the little Milton was able to grasp of it, seemed overwhelming. Ernst was the editor and printer of a newspaper called *Die Waffenlose Waechter*, or in English, "The Weapon-less Watchman." The newspaper was half in English and half in German, which was widely spoken by the Mennonites and Amish—another Christian com-munity—throughout the area. Although Milton had some understanding of German when it was spoken, he could not read the language. Learning to read English had been challenge enough for him.

The newspaper consisted of eight pages and was produced weekly, though that hardly seemed enough time for all the things Sam told Milton he would have to do. Milton tried to take it all in as Sam showed him how each letter had to be plucked from a box of cast-metal type and laid out on a compos-ing stick to form the words and lines of text to be printed. The type box had special sections for capital letters, small letters, fancy letters, and punctuation marks so tiny that Milton could hardly make them out. When several lines of type were properly arranged on the composing stick, they were transferred to a forme. Slowly the forme was filled up until it contained all the type to be printed on a particular page of the newspaper. Since *Die Waffenlose Waechter* consisted of eight pages, the process would have to be repeated eight times until all the type for each page of the newspaper had been set.

Larger type, or point sizes, had to be used for the headings, and another kind of type was to be used for bold lettering. Then there were various fonts for different shapes of letters for different headline elements such as italics. To make matters worse for Milton, the type had to be set backward in the forme so that when its mirror image was printed onto a sheet of paper, the text would appear the right way around. Once the type for a complete page had been set, a copy of it was made and proofread and any mistakes corrected before the forme was ready to be used to print the newspaper.

As Milton listened and watched his new boss demonstrate the art of typesetting, he fought the urge to cry. He wished he were back at school. At least there he could sit quietly in the back row and daydream.

Once Sam had set the type for the first page of the next issue of the newspaper, he carried the forme to the printing press and laid it on the bed of the press. Milton watched closely as his new boss inked the type, inserted a sheet of paper, and stood heavily on a treadle. The printing press seemed to burst to life. A large flywheel at the side began to turn, and the top plate of the press closed on the bottom plate where the forme sat, squeezing the paper against the inked type. As the flywheel continued to turn in response to Sam's treadling, the top plate lifted. Sam snatched the printed sheet of paper from the press and quickly inserted another before the top plate again closed. After he had printed several pages, Sam stopped treadling and triumphantly held up a printed newspaper page. Milton tried to smile as he wondered how he could possibly follow all the exact steps Mr. Ernst had shown him to produce something he had no interest in reading.

As the weeks went by, Milton tried hard to follow instructions. Sam watched over his every move and yelled if he made a mistake. Sometimes he got out his cane and took a few lashes at Milton for his mistakes. This only made Milton more nervous the next time he tried to do the same thing. To make matters worse, Milton lived in a lean-to attached to the house, and so he was never far from Mr. Ernst's watchful gaze. He was expected to work hard from sunup to sundown. And when he annoyed his employer too much, Milton was sent out to milk the Ernsts' cows or cut down thistles on their farm. Even though Milton did not want to be a farmer, he was grateful when this happened, as it gave him some time to be alone and away from Sam's volatile temper.

About six weeks after Milton had been hired as an apprentice, things came to a head. Milton had taken most of the morning laboriously picking metal letters from the type case to set a page of type in German for printing. Setting type in German was particularly difficult for Milton, who would triple-check every word to make sure he had spelled things correctly. Once he had set an entire page of type, he would lift the forme to carry it to the printing press, where Mr. Ernst would make a proof copy of it. On this particular day, just as Milton was about to set the forme down, he tripped on the corner of a mat, and the type went flying in all directions.

Sam spun around. Milton could see the veins in his neck pulsating. His eyes bulged. "Gedt oudt!" he yelled in his thick German accent. "Gedt oudt, you imbecile!"

Before he thought about it, Milton sprinted out the door of the print shop. He kept running until the Ernst house was far behind him. Then he slowed to a walk, wondering what was going to happen next. He knew that because he was an apprentice, Mr. Ernst had the right to punish him for being careless, but it hardly seemed fair. Milton was doing his best, but it just wasn't good enough.

Once he reached home, Milton got no sympathy from his father. "I'll go and talk to Sam right now," Henry fumed. "He's taken my money, and now he has to turn you into a printer."

As Milton listened to his father's horse gallop away, his heart sank. He was sure there was no way out. And he was right. An hour later his father arrived home. "Get on back there," he told Milton. "Sam says he'll have you back, but you have to try harder. None of this daydreaming. Keep your mind on your work at all times."

"Yes, Father," Milton said, eyeing his mother. He was sure he could see a tear on her cheek.

Back at the print shop, Milton made it through the rest of the week without any disasters, but he was very depressed. It would take him five years to become a printer, and he was sure that once he had finished his apprenticeship, he would never again want to look at a piece of metal type, a sheet of paper, or a printing press. He hated the way the printer's ink stained his hands and clothes. He wanted to do something different, though he had no idea what that might be.

The following Monday morning, Sam became particularly angry with Milton for overinking the printing plate and blurring a run of the newspaper's front page. The paper was supposed to be ready for sale the next morning. Sam sent Milton out to help his wife milk the cows. While he sat on the three-legged stool listening to the rhythmic swishing of the milk squirting into the pail, Milton made up his mind. He was done with printing, apprenticeship or not.

When he had finished milking the cows, Milton went back to the print shop, adjusted the felt hat on his head, and set to work.

"Pump the treadle for me, boy," Sam ordered. "That's something you can't mess up."

Milton took a deep breath as he started to pump the treadle with his right leg. Then, when his employer turned his back to check on how the printed pages were drying, Milton leaned over the printing press, tapped the hat off his head, and watched it fall into the machinery. There was a clanking noise and everything stopped.

Sam whipped around. "You clumsy oaf!" he yelled. "You've ruined the plate. This time you're fired! Get out and don't come back. Tell your father you are useless!"

Once again Milton ran out the door of the print shop, only this time he was certain he would not be back. Even his father couldn't talk his way out of this one.

When Milton arrived home, only his mother and Aunt Mattie were there. He wanted to explain to them just how unhappy he had been, but he didn't need to. The women understood that printing was not a good fit for Milton. And Milton was sure that by the time his father got home, his mother and aunt would take his side.

Henry argued with his wife, but she was firm. "Milton is not right for printing and newspapers. He needs to be making something, something he likes. Something that will earn him a good living."

"That's right," Aunt Mattie interjected. "The boy's smart enough. He just wasn't made to be a scholar, that's all. There has to be something else he will be better at."

As Henry glared at his wife and sister-in-law, Milton could see that his father was cornered. Now his fate rested in the women's hands, not his father's. No one made Milton return to Sam Ernst and the print shop, and after Milton had been home for a week, his mother and Aunt Mattie came home one day looking proud of themselves.

"We've found you a spot we think you'll like," his mother said, taking off her gloves and outer bonnet. "I've put the money down and signed the papers. You are going to work for Mr. Joseph Royer and learn the confectionery trade."

"You mean work at Joe Royer's Ice Cream Parlor and Garden in Lancaster?" Milton asked.

"Yes. You will learn how to make all those delicious candies and cakes."

"It's women's work," Henry growled, looking up from a book he was reading.

"No, it is not!" Aunt Mattie retorted. "Joe Royer earns a good living making confectioneries, and he's a man. I think Milton will be perfect for the job, and there are plenty of young people around to keep him company."

"He would have done better to be a printer," Milton's father grumbled before going back to reading his book.

"It's settled anyway," Milton's mother said. Turning to Milton, she added, "You start on Monday. You will be staying in a room in the Royer house and be expected to do everything Mr. Royer tells you to do."

Milton was too excited to sleep when night fell. He tried to recall every detail of the Ice Cream Parlor and Garden in Lancaster. Aunt Mattie had taken him there several times on Saturday afternoons for ice cream and sponge cake with lemon icing. Milton got a little nervous thinking about mixing up giant batches of nougat and peanut brittle, but then he calmed himself down. He would be an apprentice for four years—he wasn't expected to know everything the day he began the job. He would have time to learn all of the recipes and techniques of candy making, with lots of delicious samples to eat along the way. Milton drifted off to sleep with a smile on his face.

Chapter 5

A Natural

Milton jumped down from his Uncle Abraham Snavely's buggy and found himself standing on West King Street in Lancaster, right outside Royer's Ice Cream Parlor and Garden. The store was a three-story, redbrick building with double-wide plate-glass windows facing the street. The green-and-white marquee that shaded the windows proclaimed: The Coolest Spot in Lancaster—Best Ice Cream and Ice Cream Soda in the Market.

Fanny and Aunt Mattie climbed down from the buggy while Uncle Abraham hitched the horse. "I think this will suit you much better, Milton," his mother said. "You can learn to make something everyone loves. I've heard that Mr. Royer is a fair employer."

Milton smiled. As long as Joseph Royer did not have a violent temper like Sam Ernst, he would be happy. A young boy stepped outside to sweep the sidewalk. "Morning," he said.

Milton's mother nodded. "Is Mr. Royer in?"

"Yes, ma'am," the boy replied as Milton studied him. He was the same height as Milton, a little stockier, and wore a spotless white apron that fell below his knees. Milton could hardly wait to put on his own white apron and get started.

Milton held the door as his mother and aunt entered the ice cream parlor. The smell of coconut squares filled the room. "Good morning, Mrs. Hershey," Mr. Royer said. He was just as Milton remembered him—a tall, dark man with an easy manner.

Fanny asked a few questions while Milton stood quietly. As it turned out, Joseph Royer had no more room to board his apprentices and suggested that Milton seek board at the Red Lion Hotel, just a block down the street.

The rest of the afternoon Milton spent settling into the hotel, not that there was much for him to do. He had two spare changes of clothes in his suitcase, two towels, his Bible, and little else. Joseph had explained that Milton was expected to work at least twelve hours a day and more on Friday and Saturday nights when the Fulton Opera House, located around the corner, was at its busiest. There would be little time for anything else. Milton was relieved when he learned that he would start out as an errand boy, delivering boxes of cakes and sweets to customers in their homes. This meant he would be able to plan his route through the Saturday meat and produce market, the place where his mother came to sell eggs and vegetables. It comforted Milton to know that he would be able to see his mother and other familiar farmers, even if it was only for a brief moment.

Milton had difficulty sleeping the first night. He was excited about starting his new job in the morning and had never slept in a city like Lancaster before. The noise of trains passing through town, horses and buggies in the street, and voices in conversation drifted in through his open window. Still, he awoke early and dressed for work. It was fun walking down the busy street to the ice cream parlor. Shops were opening for business, and storekeepers were sweeping the sidewalk while barrels of beer were being delivered to the hotel.

At the front door of Royer's Ice Cream Parlor and Garden, Milton stopped for a moment and took a deep breath. The bell on the parlor door clanged as he opened the door. "You're early," he heard Joseph say. And with a smile Joseph added, "A good sign. Now, let's see if you are clean and ready for work."

Milton was surprised. No one had checked him for cleanliness before, but then it made sense. He was not on the farm or in a print shop anymore. He was about to become a candy maker, and cleanliness was important.

"Put out your hands," Mr. Royer said.

Milton held out his hands, palms down, so his new employer could see his fingernails.

"Good," Mr. Royer said. "Keep your nails trimmed, and wash your hands frequently. Remember, cleanliness is next to godliness."

Milton nodded. His mother often told him the same thing.

Next, Joseph gave Milton a new white apron. "Keep it spotless. The public wants to see that you care about the details, lad."

Milton nodded again as he tied the apron strings behind his back. As he looked around, he realized that everything about the ice cream parlor was spotless, from the floor to the brightly painted ceiling. Even the plants in the garden out back where patrons liked to sit on warm summer days were immaculately weeded and neatly trimmed. Milton was glad his mother had taught him how to clean and keep things tidy.

Two more boys arrived for work and stretched out their hands for inspection. Milton soon learned that Mr. Royer kept a constant watch over everyone and everything to make sure it was perfectly clean at all times.

Being a confectioner's apprentice was not quite what Milton had expected. It felt a lot like being a kitchen hand. Milton's first jobs, besides that of errand boy, involved waiting on tables, bussing and wiping down the tables, sweeping the sidewalk outside the ice cream parlor, cleaning the windows, and mopping the floor. He barely went back to the kitchen, but when he did, it was to wash a giant pile of dirty dishes. Still, Milton was happy. There were so many things to like about living in Lancaster. The town was booming after the lean economic years of the Civil War. New businesses and stores were opening in town, and existing businesses were expanding. New houses were also being built all over town, many of them mansions for the city's wealthi-est residents. All in all, Lancaster was a lively place to live.

On Prince Street, just around the corner from Royer's Ice Cream Parlor and Garden, was the Fulton Opera House. Milton attended lectures and plays there on his days off. One man he went to hear at the opera house was the up-and-coming writer and humorist Mark Twain. Milton particularly enjoyed this event as the writer recounted all sorts of humor-ous anecdotes about his recent adventures out West. Mark Twain described his ill-fated attempts at pros-pecting for gold and his life in the silver mines.

As he listened, Milton was surprised at how much Mark Twain sounded like his own father. Mil-ton was no longer sure where his father was. Henry had moved off the Nine Points farm and gone west to seek his fortune. Fanny had also moved—right into the Red Lion Hotel with her son. Milton did not mind too much. He was now sixteen years old and was glad to have company as well as someone to take care of his laundry and keep his room tidy.

As time passed at the ice cream parlor, Milton got to know the regular customers and would have their favorite ice cream and sodas waiting for them when they arrived. The ice cream parlor custom-ers fascinated him. They were a mixture of humble, Saturday-market farming folk and sophisticated city dwellers. Milton particularly remembered one woman who made him laugh harder than he had in his entire life. The middle-aged Amish woman had stepped into the ice cream parlor and looked around before walking toward the wall at the far end, which was covered in floor-to-ceiling mirrors. Suddenly she stopped and exclaimed, "Ah, Fanny, I didn't know you were in town too!"

As Milton watched, he laughed out loud. No one else was in the room; the woman was talking to her own reflection. Milton knew that as an Amish woman, she did not have mirrors in her home and had most likely never deliberately stared into one and so could not tell her own likeness. As Milton laughed, the woman turned to glare at him. Not wanting to appear rude, he explained to the woman that it was not her friend Fanny she had greeted but herself, reflected in the mirror. Soon the woman was laughing too.

Every night Milton described what he had done at work that day and noticed that as he did so, his mother became increasingly frustrated. "I paid good money for you to learn the confectioner's trade, not spend your time wiping tables and talking with customers," she grumbled. The situation came to a head one night when Milton returned to the Red Lion Hotel exhausted. He had spent the last two hours turning the crank on the ice cream machine. It was backbreaking work, especially for Milton, who was still small for his age.

"That does it!" his mother snapped. "It's time you got on with the business of candy making. I'm coming to work with you tomorrow morning."

And she did. By afternoon Milton had been promoted to the kitchen. It was time for him to learn how to make lemon drops, bonbons, rock candy, nougat, and taffy.

Milton soon discovered that cooking candy meant working with heat. It all started with water and sugar boiled together in large copper kettles. Mr. Royer explained that water boiled at a temperature of 212 degrees Fahrenheit, but when a large quantity of sugar was added, the boiling point rose to 330 degrees. To get the liquid to that temperature, several gas jets that hissed and spat blue flame were used to heat the kettles. Joseph warned Milton to be very careful when mixing and heating the sugar-and-water mixture. If any of the scalding viscous liquid splashed or spilled onto the skin, it would stick and cause a serious burn.

To his surprise, Milton learned that his employer did not use exact recipes for the various candies he made. Instead, things tended to be done by guesswork and a lot of tasting to determine the right balance of ingredients.

The most important part of the process after the sugar and water had been brought to a boil and other ingredients added was the "crack"—the exact point at which the mixture in the kettle was about to reach the perfect consistency. When the crack was reached, the gooey liquid had to be tipped from the cauldron onto trays to cool. No thermometers were used. It was left to the instinct and expertise of the particular candy maker. Milton had good instincts to know exactly when the crack was and when to pour out the kettle. (If the confectioner guessed too late, the liquid would quickly thicken in the kettle, become difficult to pour, and would need to be thrown out.) If the mixture was taffy, it would be left to cool on the trays and then draped on hooks, where it was pulled and stretched until it achieved the proper airy consistency. As Milton soon discovered, pulling taffy was very hard work. When the various candies had cooled and set, they were cut into individual pieces that were wrapped and taken to the front of the ice cream parlor for sale.

As time went on, Milton found that he loved to experiment with new recipes. He dreamed them up in his head and tried them out to see whether or not they worked. Some did and some did not, but Milton learned from every experiment he tried and was soon very proficient at making various confections. In fact, Mr. Royer called Milton a natural. How different his employer's response was from that of Sam Ernst at the print shop, who told Milton he was useless. Even when Milton did make a blunder, Mr. Royer didn't lose his temper. One time Milton forgot to turn off the fan cooling a batch of freshly roasted peanuts. Milton did not discover his mistake until after attending a performance at the Fulton Opera House with some friends. As he rounded the corner on his way home, he discovered peanut shells falling like snow in front of the ice cream parlor, blown out of an upstairs window by the still running fan.

From time to time, Milton would receive letters from his father. The letters were filled with wild tales from as far west as Colorado. Milton did not show his mother the letters; he knew they would make her angry. Even though many women would have divorced a husband who did not provide for them, Fanny Hershey would not hear of taking such an action. As a devout Mennonite, to do so would be against her religion. Thankfully, though, Aunt Mattie had moved to Lancaster, and Milton and his mother now lived with her in a modest house. Unlike his mother, Aunt Mattie had a shrewd business sense, and Milton found himself relying heavily upon her for advice.

It was Aunt Mattie who planted the idea in Milton of going into business for himself. "Once you've finished your apprenticeship, you'll know all that Mr. Royer has to teach you. Then it will be time to find out what you don't know for yourself. Start your own small business, learn from your mistakes, and find a niche that no one else is filling. That's how you'll get ahead," she told her nephew.

Milton was excited by the idea. He did not want to be an employee his whole life. With hard work and knowledge of the confectioner's trade, Milton hoped to one day have a grand store like Joseph Royer's or, perhaps with a little added luck, a string of three or four such establishments.

In early 1876, at the age of eighteen, Milton's apprenticeship at Royer's Ice Cream Parlor and Garden was complete. He was ready to go into business for himself. Aunt Mattie offered to loan Milton $150 to start his own candy-making business, and Milton knew just where he wanted it to be. He would leave his farming roots and rural Pennsylvania behind. His sights were set on Philadelphia.

Chapter 6

Wholesale and Retail Confectioner

It had been a long day for Milton. He'd started at morning loading candy-making equipment and his belongings onto Uncle Abraham's farm wagon. Uncle Abe's ten-year-old son, Stoner Snavely, had helped out where he could. Milton had invited Stoner to spend the summer with him and help him set up his new enterprise. Once the wagon was loaded, they headed off down the Lancaster Pike, the two Percheron horses clopping along slowly. The horses were more used to pulling a plow than a wagon and had sixty miles to travel before reaching their destination.

Milton did not mind the long ride atop the hard, wooden seat. In fact, he couldn't help but hum as he sat beside Uncle Abraham, who was holding

the reigns. He was on his way to the second largest city in the United States. That alone meant that
there would be over eight hundred thousand potential customers for his confections. Better yet, it was
spring 1876, and Philadelphia was on the eve of cel-
ebrating the one-hundred-year anniversary of the
signing of the Declaration of Independence in the
city. In honor of this anniversary, the Centennial
International Exhibition was being held in Philadelphia to showcase all the wonderful innovations and
advances in the United States since that time.

This was Milton's second visit to the city. The first
had been two weeks before in the company of Aunt
Mattie, who had helped Milton rent a modest building and plan out where the kettles and ovens should
go. Milton was glad for the advice of his no-nonsense
aunt. Otherwise, he might have been overcome by
the sheer size of Philadelphia. He had thought Lancaster was large, but it was nothing compared to the
size of Philadelphia. The streets were lined with brick
and stone houses and were clogged with horses and
wagons and people. Everywhere Milton looked, there
seemed to be a bustle of activity and excitement.

Once he had established his business in Philadelphia, Milton hoped to be able to take some time
to visit the Centennial International Exhibition. He
was particularly interested in seeing the large Corliss
steam engine on display in the enormous Machinery
Building and the various devices it could power. For
now, Milton had to put ideas of visiting the exhibition aside. His job was to get his confectionery business up and running so he could take advantage of

the pennies jingling in the pockets of the carefree crowds visiting the exhibition during the six months it was open.

Evening was settling over the city by the time the Percherons pulled the wagon to a halt in front of 935 Spring Garden Street, between the Schuylkill and Delaware Rivers. This was the place Aunt Mattie had helped Milton rent two weeks before. The location was close to Fairmount Park, where the Centennial International Exhibition would be held. Milton wasted no time in getting to work. The kettles and stove were moved into the basement, where Milton rigged up an exhaust pipe out onto the street in front of the building. He imagined the beguiling smell of candy wafting into the noses of hungry passersby. Milton realized, however, that it was going to be some time before he would be selling candy from a store. His first job was to find a way to sell candy directly to those attending the exhibition when it opened.

Milton took remarkably little time to get his candy production up and running. He installed a taffy hook and taught Stoner how to pull the taffy to the right consistency and to cut and wrap the caramel candies Milton made. Once the candy-making process was under way, Milton turned his attention to finding customers. He rented a pushcart in anticipation of the May 10 opening of the Centennial International Exhibition. Milton was out in the street with his pushcart selling candy to the crowd when the city's bells rang at nine o'clock in the morning, announcing the opening of the show gates. The weather was overcast, but that did not stop over one hundred thousand people from thronging into the Centennial International Exhibition to see President Ulysses Grant, accompanied by Brazilian Emperor Dom Pedro, open the event.

As the crowd swelled through the gates, Milton caught sight of the Main Exhibition Building, a huge structure made of iron and brick that enclosed twenty acres of exhibit space. Beyond he could see fantastical towers and minarets rising high into the air. Milton looked forward to the time when he would go through the gates and view the 285 acres of exhibits and grounds.

Although Milton's candy sales were good that first day, hundreds of other candy sellers were also peddling their wares. Milton needed to find a way to distinguish himself from the other candy peddlers in the area. He began by designing his own business card and having it printed. One side of the card featured a drawing of Machinery Hall, along with the dimensions of the hall: 1402 feet long by 360 feet wide. On the other side of the card were the words, "M. S. Hershey, Wholesale and Retail Confectioner." Milton hoped that people would keep the business card as a souvenir of the exhibit and as a reminder to choose Hershey confections.

Within weeks Milton was so busy selling candy in the streets around the Centennial International Exhibition that he asked his mother to join him. She did, renting a house on Ridge Avenue. Soon afterward, Stoner had to return to his father's farm, and an unlikely person pitched in to help Milton. Harry Lebkicher, or Lebbie, as everyone called him, had been a lumberyard worker in Lancaster and was an old family friend. Milton, his mother, and Lebbie were kept busy working around the clock to keep up the supply of caramels and sweets to sell. Milton also hired a team of eager boys to sell his candies from baskets to supplement his efforts with the pushcart.

Milton did manage to find the time to visit the exhibition. The main exhibition hall was massive inside, with row upon row of exhibits from the United States and around the world. Milton loved Machinery Hall, where he got to see the Corliss steam engine. The steam engine was forty-five feet tall, had a flywheel that was thirty feet in diameter, and produced fourteen hundred horsepower. In fact, through a system of shafts that stretched for over a mile, the Corliss steam engine was being used to power many of the exhibits.

Another exhibit that caught Milton's attention was the right arm and hand holding a torch from a large statue named *Liberty* that was being made by French sculptor Frédéric-Auguste Bartholdi. The statue would eventually stand on an island in New York City's harbor. For fifty cents you could climb a ladder to the balcony on which the flame of the torch sat and get a bird's-eye view of the Centennial International Exhibition. As he took in the attractions, Milton wondered where his father was. He knew a place like this would spark a thousand ideas in Henry Hershey.

The Centennial International Exhibition closed on November 10, 1876. In the six months it had been open, about ten million people, 20 percent of the population of the United States, had been through its gates.

Milton returned the pushcart and began to concentrate on opening a storefront business. He moved down the street to a larger building and set up shop. His mother was the main saleswoman and wrapped candies when the store was not busy. Milton and Lebbie handled everything else: buying ingredients, cooking, pulling taffy, cutting the various candies, and, now that Milton had a proper store, making ice cream.

Always ready to try something new, Milton looked for things that would attract customers to his business. One summer night he hired a German band to play outside the store. When a crowd gathered to listen to the band, he offered his refreshing ice cream for sale for five cents a plate. It was such a successful experiment that he hired the band several more times over the summer. Another time he added short poems inside the candy wrappers and called the combination French Secrets.

Although Milton was certain that everyone involved with the enterprise was working hard and that sales were good, he found it difficult to make much money. In fact, some weeks he lost money. Milton puzzled over how this could be. He realized that it was difficult to make a profit from penny candies when the price of sugar kept rising. In the fall of 1878 Aunt Mattie visited Milton. He was both relieved and embarrassed to see her. Milton admitted that he had run out of money and urgently needed four hundred dollars. Aunt Mattie did not have that much money on her, but she agreed to write to her brother Abraham and have him send the money to Milton.

Milton hoped it would be the last time he would ever have to ask for money for his business. Unfortunately it was not. Over the next year he had to ask for small amounts of money to keep his business afloat. Often the other stores that stocked Milton's candy owed him money, yet the big supply companies would not allow him to buy sugar on credit. This created a cash shortage, causing Milton to have to ask for money from his family. As much as he hated to do it, in December 1880 he had to write to Uncle Abraham with another request.

Dear Uncle,

I am sorry to bother you but cannot well do without as it takes so much money. Just now Aunt [Mattie] wishes you to send 600 [dollars] . . . and she will stand good for it. She just wants it till the first of the year, so you will greatly oblige me by [sending] it as [soon] as possible on Monday and do not fail as it will save us some trouble.

Yr. Respct Nephew
Milt

Milton's stomach was continually twisted in knots over money issues in his business. Almost every month he had to write, asking for more money to tide him over while he collected what was owed him and bought sugar to make more candy.

Despite the difficulties, Milton and his team continued to work. This was disrupted early in 1881 when Henry Hershey showed up unexpectedly. Milton's mother and aunt gave Henry a cool reception, but Milton was delighted to see his father again. His father's youthful optimism had something appealing about it, and Milton certainly needed someone optimistic at his side.

"Enough of this small-time candy making!" his father exclaimed. "If you want to make big money, you have to do things in a big way!"

Milton soon learned that his father had notions about joining him in business and expanding to include manufacturing and selling transportation and exhibit cases. Henry had arrived with two of these creations: beautifully handcrafted wood and glass cases that fit together to form a long display case with adjustable partitions in which to put candy or other small goods. The display cases were made to sit on top of a counter, allowing the storekeeper to access the goods they contained from behind. Milton thought the cases were a great idea. He just wasn't sure they were the right thing for him to be selling. Still, his father's enthusiasm overcame his better judgment, and soon father and son were in business together.

Henry also insisted they make and sell cough drops called HHH Medicated Cough Drops. The cough drops were not as popular as candy, but Milton hoped they would help to get him out of his financial hole. This was not to be. After the return of his father, Milton found the balance of his bank account plummeting even farther. This time his Snavely relatives were not willing to bail him and his father out. Henry had burned any bridges of loyalty to the Snavely clan years before.

Milton secretly wanted to see his parents get back together, but instead they bickered constantly. Eventually Aunt Mattie and his mother came to him with an ultimatum, "Either Henry Hershey leaves or we do. You make the choice."

Milton was heartbroken and exhausted from working twenty hours a day to try to keep his business afloat. Suddenly nothing seemed to matter. He felt confused and could not think straight. Milton's mother bundled him off to bed, telling her son that he would feel better in the morning. But he did not. He felt worse, much worse. He knew that he could not get out of bed and face the day. He was worn out. Milton stayed in bed for most of November and on into December. He knew that his mother, Lebbie, and Aunt Mattie were doing most of the work to keep the business going, but he could not find the energy to care. All he wanted to do was sleep until the problems went away.

By Christmas Milton felt well enough to take up the reins of his business. His father had grown restless while Milton was ill and announced that he was heading west. "I'm off to make a claim in the Rockies," he told Milton. "Close this place down and join me. There's gold there, I know it."

Milton said farewell to his father and tried hard

to concentrate on his candy business, but it was not easy. Although he wrote more letters asking for money, in his heart he knew it was over. He was a failure as a business owner. After a dreary Christmas, Milton wrote to Uncle Abraham asking for one last favor: to bring his wagon to Philadelphia to collect the confectionery equipment.

Stoner Snavely, who was now sixteen years old, and his brother Rohrer arrived in the city with the horses and wagon and set about helping Milton dismantle his kitchen and load it onto the wagon. Then they drove to the house, where Aunt Mattie and Milton's mother pointed out the few things they wanted to take with them.

Before he knew it, Milton was sitting on the wagon, wedged between his two cousins. He watched as the Percherons clopped along the Lancaster Pike. He had set out for Philadelphia six years before filled with hope and promise. Now he was headed back to Lancaster County without success. And while he puzzled over what had gone wrong in Philadelphia, the real puzzle was what he would do next. Moving on to a new part of the country might give him a fresh start.

Chapter 7

Wandering

Milton picked up the April 5, 1882, edition of the *Rocky Mountain News*. The bold headline across the front page declared, "Jesse James Shot to Death by Man Named Ford." Milton quickly read about how the famous outlaw had been shot to death by a member of his own gang in St. Joseph, Missouri.

"It makes you think," Milton said to his father, who was enjoying a bowl of oatmeal.

"Think what?" Henry replied.

"It makes you think a man should have a gun if he lives in the West. Out here in Denver it's not like back east. I think I might buy myself a gun today."

His father nodded. "Not a bad idea, son. Silver fever brings out the worst in some men, that's for sure."

As Milton read the rest of the newspaper, he reassured himself that owning a gun would be a good thing. He had been in Denver for a week now, and it was hard—much harder than his father had suggested in his letters—to find a job. At first Milton thought he would be able to find work with a candy maker, but no one seemed to want to hire a young professional like him. There were too many despondent men who were done with prospecting for silver and were willing to stir batches of sugar and flavoring for just pennies an hour.

Milton sighed. He knew he would have to broaden his search and accept any job he could find. He was grateful to still have the hundred dollars, a gift from Aunt Mattie, that his mother had sewn into the hem of his jacket. "It's for emergencies," she had said. Milton knew she meant the kind of emergency where he would need to get on a train and head back to Lancaster County, Pennsylvania. But he was determined to stay with his father and make a new life for himself in the West.

After breakfast Milton visited a hardware store and bought a Starr revolver. He didn't like the idea of carrying a gun around, but Jesse James's death had spooked him into thinking he needed protection, or at least to make it look like he had protection. In fact, Milton did not buy any ammunition to go with the pistol. He trusted that if he needed to draw his gun, doing so would be enough to get him out of any difficult situation.

With his new pistol tucked into his belt, Milton set out for another day of looking for work. As he wandered the back alleys of Denver, he saw a sign in the window of a house that read "Young Man

Wanted." Milton decided to find out what kind of a job it might be. He knocked on the door, and a voice from inside bellowed, "Come in."

Milton turned the door handle and stepped inside. The door slammed shut and was locked behind him. "I need work. What sort of job do you have?" he asked the old man standing beside the now locked front door.

"Go in there," the man said, pointing to the door across the room.

A little suspicious, Milton walked over and opened the door. Inside the room a group of bedraggled young men were huddled together. Suddenly Milton knew why the old man had locked the door behind him. It wasn't to keep people from getting in but to keep them from getting out. The young men huddled in the room were going to be sent to some sort of labor camp. Milton had read in the newspaper about this growing practice. Down-on-their-luck young men were lured with the promise of jobs and then sent to labor camps, where they were forced to work around the clock for a pittance, with no chance of escape.

Milton spun around. "Let me out of here now," he demanded.

The old man just laughed. "Get on in there, boy," he said.

Panicked by the situation he had gotten himself into, Milton suddenly recalled the Starr revolver in his belt. With a flick of his wrist he pulled it from his waistband, where it had been hidden by his coat. He aimed the gun at the old man and repeated himself. "Now let me out of here."

Without a word, the old man walked over and unlocked the front door. Milton bounded through the door as soon as it opened. Outside Milton hurried away from the house, feeling lucky to be free and still with the hundred dollars sewn into his jacket. As he regained his composure, he chuckled to himself, thinking how the unloaded pistol had fooled the old man.

After this experience Milton decided to listen to his father's advice. Even though Henry's advice had often led Milton astray, this time Milton found it to be sensible. "You need to find the confectionery kitchens that are servicing the mining camps and cattle stations. I've seen them out there, wagons filled with victuals [food] and supplies heading out of town. Someone is making candy for those supply trips, I can guarantee it. That's where you'll find work."

Based on this advice, Milton searched harder for confectioners in town and located a one-man business making caramels to be sold out of town. Milton showed the owner his completed apprenticeship papers and was hired on the spot.

The confectionery shop was not as well organized or as clean as Joseph Royer's had been back in Lancaster, but Milton soon found his rhythm. On his first day at the new job, he discovered something odd. Mr. Whiting, the shop's owner, did not add paraffin to the caramels he made. Paraffin wax, made from petroleum, was normally used to help set the caramel candies and make them chewy. Milton had never heard of a caramel recipe that did not include it. "What makes the caramels chewy if you don't use paraffin?" he asked.

Mr. Whiting smiled. "A secret I found out a long time ago—milk, fresh whole milk. I add it to the mixture and boil it all up together. The customers like the way it feels in their mouth, and it doesn't stick to their teeth. Best of all, the caramels last for weeks, even months in winter, without losing their flavor."

Milton frowned. "How is that possible? Caramels made with paraffin last only two or three days. Why, during the Centennial International Exhibition in Philadelphia I had to make them every night. It was very hot, and they spoiled quickly."

"Somehow using milk just works." Mr. Whiting reached over to a jar. "Here, try one of these. It's been in that jar since Christmas."

Milton unwrapped the caramel candy and held it to his nose. It smelled sweet. Then he popped it in his mouth. As he chewed he found the flavor wonderful—subtle and buttery. "Perfect," he said, shaking his head. "I've learned something today. I would never have thought of adding milk to caramels. In fact, I don't think anyone but you ever has."

Milton soon mastered the art of making the delicious, long-lasting caramel treats. He worked hard for Mr. Whiting, cooking up batches of caramel in large kettles, waiting for the crack before pouring the mixture out and cooling it. Then, as with taffy, he threw the cooled mixture over a hook and pulled it repeatedly until the caramel reached the right airy consistency. Even with using milk instead of paraffin in the mixture, pulling was still the most exhausting part of the process. Once the caramel had reached the right consistency, Milton laid it out on long trays to set before cutting it into pieces and wrapping the pieces individually. Milton worked hard, but he was content. He was earning a living. But things were getting tougher in Denver. As fall approached, his father decided to move on. "Boom times are over here, lad," Henry told Milton. "I hear Chicago's the place to be."

Milton had expected this. By now he accepted the fact that his father would never settle down in any one place. The grass would always seem greener somewhere else.

Henry urged his son to go with him, but when Milton refused, Henry boarded the train for Chicago alone. Milton was lonely without his father. Over the next several weeks he thought hard about his future. Could he really make his fortune—or even a good living—in Denver? He doubted it. By November he had packed up his few possessions and followed his father to Chicago. As the train moved along and the spectacular scenery of the Rocky Mountains receded, Milton felt like a failure. He was on the move to a new city without much to show for his past year of work. Or so he thought.

Once the train pulled into Chicago, Milton set out to find his father. He had the address of a boarding house, and as he made his way there, he was surprised by what he saw. Even though Chicago had a population of half a million people, it was nothing like Philadelphia or even Denver. In Denver they had electric power and a beautiful opera house. But Chicago was dirty and spread out. The smell of cattle permeated the air, and a chilly wind blew off Lake Michigan.

Milton found his father to be just as incorrigible as ever. Henry had set himself up as a carpenter and was building bars for saloons in town. Thankfully he made enough money to help Milton buy supplies to set up his own small taffy and caramel business. Just as he had done in Philadelphia, Milton made and wrapped candies by night and sold them from a cart during the day. The work was hard and tiring, and his father helped out when he could. Regrettably, Henry had cosigned a loan for a friend, and when the friend did not pay back the loan, the bank came after Henry for the balance. This wiped out all the money both Milton and his father had accumulated. Once again they looked for a fresh start. Henry had heard about opportunities in Louisiana, and the two men boarded a train for New Orleans.

Money was tight, and the pair could afford only a cheap flophouse in New Orleans. Within a week, Milton wondered what he had been thinking, allowing his father to talk him into the venture. It had been a year since he left Philadelphia and his failed candy business. In the time since then, Milton had lived in three states, covered hundreds of miles by train, and was worse off than when he started. Something had to change.

Milton did a lot of soul-searching in New Orleans and came to a startling conclusion. He would move one more time, not to some boomtown where money could be lost more easily than gained, but to the largest, most established city in the United States—New York.

With his last few dollars, Milton bought a ticket back to Lancaster. He wanted to see his mother and Aunt Mattie again, and just as important, he needed their financial backing. He hoped they would forgive him for following his father around the country.

Back home in the rolling green countryside around Lancaster, Milton did not talk much about his father. To do so would inflame the situation and make it unlikely that Aunt Mattie would loan him any more money. Instead, he told his aunt and mother all about the new ingredient for caramel and how milk had made the candies last longer and taste better. The two women caught Milton's enthusiasm, and Aunt Mattie agreed to loan him some more money—not enough to start his own business again, but enough to get him to New York City and rent a room. The plan was for him to work for an established confectioner by day and cook his own creations at night. It would require discipline and hard work, but Milton was sure he had both abilities.

Everything about moving to New York City went well. With money in his pocket, Milton confidently stepped off the ferry onto Manhattan Island. The same day, he landed a job working for Huyler's Candies, a well-known confectioner who sold bonbons and chocolates. Better yet, Milton found a room to rent that offered kitchen privileges, though he was sure the landlady could not imagine just how much use her kitchen was about to get.

Milton wrote home regularly, reporting on what he had learned. The city had about fifty candy wholesalers and hundreds of stores that sold candy. Milton also reported on his venture into chocolate making for his employer. Although Huyler's asked a high price for its chocolate, the candy was, in Milton's estimation, barely edible. The chocolate was gritty and melted quickly on warm days. One of Milton's customers brought him a chocolate candy from Switzerland that had been made by a new company called Nestlé. Milton was astonished when he tasted it. The Nestlé chocolate was smooth and creamy, unlike anything he had tried before. Milton could not figure out how this Swiss chocolate was made, but he promised himself that one day he would.

About a year after arriving in New York, Milton took a major step. He quit his job and rented space to make and sell his own candies. The spot he chose was on Sixth Avenue between Forty-second and Forty-third Streets and was nestled between a Chinese laundry and the Hippodrome Theatre. New businesses were opening up all around him, and Milton was confident that the foot traffic in front of his store would grow. In the fall of 1884 his mother and Aunt Mattie joined him in the venture. Once again the Hershey-Snavely team swung into action, cooking, pulling, cutting, wrapping, and selling caramels, taffy, candied fruit, nuts, and fruitcakes. Milton was grateful that his mother and aunt had stuck by him and hoped this time it would pay off for them all.

Somewhere in the back of his mind, Milton had the feeling that his father would show up again—as he always seemed to. And when he did show up, it usually marked the beginning of the end. Sure enough, just as the holiday season of 1884 was getting under way, Henry arrived in New York to visit Milton. His mother and aunt were not amused, and Milton's stomach twisted as he realized he would once more be caught in the middle of his parents' restless marriage.

The truth was, Milton needed an extra worker, and soon his father was helping out. Henry showed up every morning, ready to take a basket of candies several blocks to Grand Central Station to sell to train passengers. Milton was impressed with his father's meekness. Henry did not talk so much about making it big and seemed happy to fit in with the way Milton was running things.

Milton's business went well, and soon he was able to buy an old horse and dray so that he could make deliveries farther around the city. However, this came with its own set of challenges. After working most of the night, Milton was perpetually tired, and the clip-clopping of the horse's hooves on the cobblestones made Milton sleepy. On one particular day he fell asleep holding the reins. He awoke to find himself sailing through the air and into a pile of trash cans. Looking up, he saw an old man standing over him. "Those lads," the man said, shaking his head. "Nothing better to do. They threw a firecracker at your horse. Shocking what young ones will do today!"

Milton scrambled to his feet. His horse and dray were nowhere to be seen, but it was not hard to tell in which direction the animal had bolted. It had left a trail of caramels and taffies, which small children were scrambling to pick up.

Milton eventually found his horse and dray on Broadway, with all the candies gone. This was a setback for Milton, who realized he needed more sleep. He asked his father to take over the deliveries, which helped a little. However, Henry often read while he drove the dray, and that caused its own set of traffic jams and near misses.

Each month as Milton went over the bookkeeping, his spirits rose, so much so that a larger space on the corner of West Forty-second Street caught his eye. When the place came up for rent, he secured it, even though he still had several months to go on his old lease. Milton decided that he would sublet the old store to someone else, but this proved harder than he thought. He was left paying the rent on two stores, which left him with no money to buy the larger equipment he needed to make his next product—cough drops.

Once again Milton's father convinced him to make cough drops, telling him that there were enough coughing and sneezing people in New York City on a winter's day to make them both rich. Milton thought his father was probably right, but he needed to invest in larger steam kettles to make such a venture profitable. Without enough money to buy the equipment, Milton was stuck, until a kitchen equipment salesman showed up at the new store and offered to sell Milton everything he needed for ten thousand dollars in credit. Although Milton did not like the idea of buying the equipment on credit, taking a loan from a manufacturing company seemed like a better option than going back to his relatives and asking for more money. Besides, he was unsure whether they would even give him more. So he signed the necessary documents for the credit, and soon the new equipment was up and running in the kitchen.

Hershey Cough Drops, the potential shining star of Milton's confectionery lineup, were a flop. They were good enough lozenges, but New Yorkers already had a favorite brand, Smith Brothers Cough Drops, and the Smith brothers sold their lozenges more cheaply than Milton could afford to sell his.

Once again, in the summer of 1886, a familiar predicament confronted Milton. He was paying the rent on two stores and feeding and housing his mother and Aunt Mattie, and soon the first payment on the equipment would be due. But he had no money with which to pay it. He stopped paying rent on the old store, and the landlord sued him for what was owed. And when he could not pay for the new kitchen equipment, the manufacturing company repossessed it.

This was the last straw. Milton told his mother and aunt about what had happened, and they managed to scrape together a few dollars between them, enough to crate up Milton's old kitchen equipment. This was loaded onto a train bound for Lancaster, designated "Collect," meaning the stationmaster in Lancaster would hold the equipment until Milton could pay the freight on it. Fanny Hershey and Aunt Mattie headed back to Pennsylvania, while Milton's father stayed in New York. Milton himself stayed in New York for a few more days to tie up loose ends. Then he made the long, painful train ride back to where he had started.

Chapter 8

The Best Caramels in America

I t was a beautiful afternoon when the train arrived in Lancaster. The sun shone from a cloudless blue sky, but even that was not enough to lift Milton's spirits. As he walked several miles along the road south from Lancaster to New Danville, where Uncle Abraham's farm was located, Milton dreaded what he had to do next. His stomach turned as he thought about the various arguments he would make to convince his uncle, a conservative Mennonite farmer, to loan him money. At the farmhouse Aunt Carrie greeted Milton as she unpinned laundry from the clothesline. "Milton, it's you. Your uncle didn't know whether you'd be out to see us or not." Her voice was flat, and Milton gauged from its tone that he was not particularly welcome. Still, he took off his hat and went inside.

Uncle Abraham was sitting at the table and barely looked up as his nephew walked in. "What is it you want?" he asked.

Milton took a deep breath and launched into his rehearsed argument for financial support. "I've learned a lot in the time I've been away, Uncle Abraham. I've seen a lot of things. I think I now know how to make the candy business work. It's not about making a whole lot of things, but making one thing well. While I was in Denver, I learned a secret recipe for making caramels. They are the best caramels I've ever tasted. Creamy, chewy, but not sticky. They last for weeks. And the best thing of all is the secret ingredient. What do you think it is?"

Uncle Abraham looked at Milton. "Don't know," he said in such a way that he could easily have added, "don't care."

Undeterred, Milton went on. "It's milk. And nothing is better than fresh milk from a Pennsylvania dairy. We have everything here to make the best caramels in America!"

"Don't use 'we' around here," Uncle Abraham said. "There's no backing for you among the Snavelys. And don't go asking your Aunt Mattie either. She's done with you, and so is your mother, though you'll never hear her say as much. We've done more than our share to see you right, but you're a Hershey, a true son of Henry—a dreamer. You'll never stick with anything long enough to make it work for you."

Milton gulped. He had suspected that his Snavely relatives had given up on him, but the words still stung. He stood up. "I guess that's all the business we have with each other today."

"I guess it is," Uncle Abraham snapped. Milton expected him to offer him dinner and a bed for the night, but his uncle's lips remained sealed.

"Good day, then," Milton said, giving his uncle one last chance.

"Good day," came the reply.

Milton picked up his hat and headed for the door just as Aunt Carrie came through it. "So you're off, are you?" she asked. Milton nodded. "Good-bye," she added.

As Milton walked back along the road to Lancaster, the sun was beginning to set. At first he felt angry that his relatives had turned their backs on him. Worse, they had compared him to his wandering father. But as he walked, Milton's burden began to lift. He felt free in a strange way. "It's all up to me now," he told himself. "I won't need much, just a small shed, a way to pay the freight on my equipment, and a whole lot of work. I'm smarter now. I know I can earn a good living making caramels."

By the time Milton got back into Lancaster, he felt much better. He would find his old friend Lebbie and see whether he had room for Milton to spend the night. Tomorrow was a new day.

After helping Milton with the business in Philadelphia, Lebbie had returned to his old job as clerk at the Lancaster lumberyard. Milton soon found him at a boarding house across the street. Lebbie did not look surprised to see Milton. And when Milton explained his situation, Lebbie set up a cot in his tiny room and bought dinner for him at the adjoining tavern. As he lay in the narrow cot that night, Milton made a promise to himself. When he became rich he would treat Lebbie right. Lebbie was a true friend when he needed one.

The next day Lebbie paid for Milton's candy-making equipment to be released from the rail freight yard. He then showed Milton a place for rent that he thought might suit his needs. "It's not much," Lebbie said as they surveyed the room in Jacob Gable's warehouse on the west side of Duke Street, "but it would be a start if you want to make those milk caramels you were telling me about last night."

"The rent's reasonable, but I don't have it," Milton said meekly.

Lebbie smiled a rare smile. "Well, lad, I'll back you. I'll pay the rent for the first three months. You'll have your equipment back and a stove in the corner. Will that be enough to get you going?"

Milton nodded gratefully. "If I can just get one batch of caramels ready to sell, I know people will buy them."

"Alright," Lebbie said. "Let's see what you can do."

Milton set right to work. His first task was to get the equipment from the railway yard to the warehouse. It was uphill, and the kettles and other pieces of equipment were large and heavy. There was no way he could drag them all to his new place alone. Then Milton remembered the horses and drays lined up outside the courthouse waiting for hauling jobs. He headed there and found a man he recognized. "Johnny Otto!" he exclaimed. "It's been a long time!"

Johnny smiled and climbed down from his dray. Milton explained that he had a hauling job but no money to pay for it until he got his new business under way. Johnny agreed to haul the equipment for Milton and collect the fifty-cent fee later.

By the end of the day Milton had accomplished far more than he had anticipated, and he was grateful to Lebbie and Johnny for their help. He felt sure this was a sign of good things to come.

It was not easy, but penny by penny Milton began to build a small caramel business. Each night he concentrated on making the best caramels he could at his room in the warehouse. This was a challenge because the coal stove had to be stoked constantly to get it up to temperature. Even then it was hard to get the kettles to the high temperature needed for caramelizing the sugar, adding the other ingredients, and stretching the mixture onto long trays to cool before pulling it. Each afternoon Milton walked out of town to buy fresh milk from a local dairy farmer. Of course, during the day he would head into the streets of Lancaster with a basket of caramels and sell them door-to-door.

Slowly Milton's mother and Aunt Mattie began to concede that the caramel business might be successful. They moved into a house nearby and returned to their roles of cutting and wrapping candy while Milton peddled it door-to-door. Milton earned enough money to buy a pushcart, which meant he could venture farther around town. But Milton soon discovered that this could mean trouble. Lancaster had a pecking order for pushcart vendors, with the most established vendors getting the best routes and busy spots to sell their wares. Milton and his caramels were not welcome in many parts of the city. One day as he pushed his cart up Cabbage Hill, he was pelted with stones. Milton turned the cart around and headed downhill fast.

As he jogged along to safety behind the cart, Milton felt discouraged. He'd tried so hard, and now locals were throwing stones at him. What could he do to make a better living? If only he had bigger kettles and a steam furnace, he could make enough caramels to sell to wholesalers and not have to spend so much time selling in the streets.

As Milton wheeled the pushcart home, he thought about the equipment he would need to make his business bigger. He calculated that it would cost about seven hundred dollars to take his caramel-making operation to the next level. First he needed a bigger facility with a steam boiler. This he found several blocks away in an old building that had once been the Edison Electric Plant. The building, owned by Jacob Gable, was on Church Street and housed a brewery, a shop that made horse-drawn carriages, and a carpet-beating business, with a piano and organ manufacturer upstairs. Milton decided the available space for rent in this building wouldn't be the quietest place for a caramel-making business, but the space was big and came with a steam boiler for heating his kettles.

Getting the seven hundred dollars he needed for more equipment was the greater challenge. Where was he going to get such a sum of money? He knew it was pointless to ask his Snavely relatives. The only other approach was getting a loan from a bank. But after talking to three different loan officers at three different banks, Milton concluded that at twenty-nine years of age, with no assets and two failed businesses behind him, he was not a good loan risk. He reminded himself and the bank loan officers that he now knew far more than before and that having failed in business twice, he was now ready to succeed. However, this line of argument did not sit well with the bankers.

With nothing to lose but his pride, Milton approached yet another bank for a loan. This time it was Lancaster National Bank, which the Snavely family frequented. Milton hoped that the bank manager would keep the conversation he was about to have confidential. He did not want to give his uncles more reason to ridicule him.

As it turned out, the bank manager was not available, so Milton explained his situation to the cashier, a young man about Milton's age named Frank Brenneman. "So you really think this will work?" Frank asked.

Milton smiled. "I think so. I've learned a lot about businesses and how not to run them. Now I think I can do it right."

Frank looked up with a questioning look on his face. "I'm not sure this loan for seven hundred dollars can go through as it stands. But if you have someone who will put up something of value—a property, for example—as a deposit, I think we might be able to do it. If I'm not mistaken, you're related to the Snavelys."

"I am," Milton replied. "But I would rather not ask them for help."

"I understand, but unless someone underwrites the loan, it won't meet our lending criteria."

Milton nodded glumly. "I'll see what I can do."

Milton sighed deeply as he left the bank. If only he could do this alone, but he could not. He went to talk to Aunt Mattie one more time, explaining that he would be responsible for the seven-hundred-dollar loan and that no matter what happened, he would pay the amount back. Aunt Mattie eventually agreed to allow Milton to use a house she owned on South Queen Street as surety to underwrite the loan.

The loan was approved, and Milton left Lancaster National Bank with seven hundred dollars, which was to be paid back in three months. With the money in hand, he rushed to buy bigger kettles and other equipment for the larger space he had rented.

Milton, his mother, and Aunt Mattie hardly slept. They worked almost around the clock making caramels in the new facility. Milton was glad he no longer had to stoke a coal stove and coax it along to get his kettles to the required temperature. Now steam from the boiler got his kettles to the right temperature in no time at all. Soon long trays of caramels were stretched out cooling and waiting to be pulled, cut, and wrapped. The aroma from the caramels drifted throughout the old building and out onto the street.

As he worked, Milton remembered the Smith Brothers Cough Drops in New York City and how once the public got that name in their heads, they did not want any other lozenges, even if they tasted better. Drawing on this experience, he decided that it would be a good idea to come up with a special name for his caramels. That way they'd stand out, helping customers tell them apart from other caramels. Milton wanted something that sounded scientific and decided Crystal A Caramels was a good fit.

As the ninety-day loan period drew to a close, Milton realized that his best effort and that of his mother and aunt had not been enough. He did not have seven hundred dollars to pay the loan back. This meant that the bank would seize Aunt Mattie's house and sell it to pay back what was owed. The very thought of this made Milton sick to his stomach, but each day he got out of bed and went on, hoping for a miracle.

Just a few days before the loan repayment was due, Milton was out selling candy from his pushcart when a man in a tweed suit purchased three pennies' worth of Crystal A Caramels. Milton watched as the man walked off, spun around, and walked back. "Did you make these, young man?" the stranger asked in a clipped English accent.

"Yes, sir," Milton replied. "They're my Crystal A's. The best caramels in America."

"I do believe they are!" the man exclaimed. "I wish they would keep fresh. I'd take some back to London with me."

"Oh, but they *will* stay fresh," Milton said with a smile. "My caramels are made with milk. That keeps them fresh for weeks, even months."

He watched as the man's eyebrows rose. "Milk? Really? Months? You're sure about that?"

"Absolutely. I guarantee it. I make them myself. How many would you like?"

The man chuckled. "That's the question, isn't it?" He thrust out his hand. "My name is Andrew Decies. As it happens, I'm a confectionery importer, and I've been looking for a consistent caramel product. I would be interested in introducing your caramels to the English market if you can guarantee me enough quantity and deliver them fresh. And if the first order arrives in good shape and sells well, I'll be ordering more, regularly."

Milton stared at the man, almost in disbelief. It was hard to take in what he was hearing. "I think I can do that," he stammered. "How many pounds of caramels are you talking about?"

For the next hour, the two men talked about the details of exporting caramels to England. Milton tried to sound confident, but his heart was racing. What was he thinking, telling Mr. Decies that he could deliver caramels to England—in six weeks! There was no way that he, his mother, and Aunt Mattie could produce that many caramels with the equipment they had. Still, Milton agreed to meet with Mr. Decies that night, where he signed a wholesale agreement. Milton was certain that if he could deliver his caramels to England, it would be the turning point in his business.

Aunt Mattie and his mother were not so enthusiastic. Milton could understand why. It meant more work for them, and Aunt Mattie did not have the cash to lend him to buy the needed equipment. She also was concerned about sending a huge order of caramels to England. What if the order did not arrive in good shape or Mr. Decies was not an honest man? Aunt Mattie shook her head. "There's a lot riding on this, Milton. I'm not sure your business is ready to grow that fast. You'll need more preparation space, more kettles, and hired help to fill an order that big."

She might as easily have added, "Remember the other times," but she did not have to. Milton was painfully aware how business deals could go wrong. But something inside said this was a good move, a once-in-a-lifetime opportunity that he should seize.

It took every ounce of Milton's courage to walk through the doors back into Lancaster National Bank. The last time, he had asked for a seven-hundred-dollar loan for ninety days. Now he was back to tell Frank Brenneman that although the ninety-day loan period was up, he could not pay back the loan. But that wasn't the worst of it. Milton was about to ask for an additional thousand dollars to be able to fill Mr. Decies's order for caramels. As he closed the door of the bank behind him, Milton whispered a prayer for help. He had no idea what was going to happen if the bank turned him down.

Chapter 9

A Successful Business

Frank greeted Milton as he walked into the bank. Milton smiled as best he could. "Please, sit down," Frank said. "I was expecting you today. I trust things have gone well."

Milton took a deep breath. "In many ways they have," he said. "In fact, I just received a very large order from England with the promise of more to come."

"Well done!" the banker replied. "I'm sure your aunt, Miss Snavely, will be glad. Do you have the money to repay the loan?"

Milton shook his head. "Unfortunately, I can't pay it back yet. I need to have it renewed. And I need to borrow a thousand dollars more to buy the necessary equipment to fill the English order."

Frank raised his eyebrows. "Oh," he said. "That's not what I had hoped to hear."

"I know, but it's the reality of the situation. I have added up the numbers." Milton pulled a black leatherbound notebook from his breast pocket and flipped it open. "If I can just have one thousand dollars more, I can hire three people and rent extra space in the building I am currently using to produce my caramels."

"I'm not sure that will be possible. It would be most irregular," Frank said.

Milton sensed the opportunity slipping away. Suddenly he had an idea. "Come with me, Mr. Brenneman. Let me show you my enterprise. Then you will have a better idea of what I am asking. I have material and merchandise. Let me show you what I have."

Much to Milton's relief, Frank agreed to go. Soon Milton was showing him around the kitchen where he produced his caramels. Seeing the facility through the banker's eyes, Milton had to admit it was not impressive. The wagon maker next door was hammering on a metal bracket, making a terrible noise that echoed throughout the building. His mother and Aunt Mattie were huddled in one corner of the room feverishly wrapping caramels. Milton pointed out the bags of sugar and several of his large kettles. "Those kettles hold only ten gallons. That's three hundred pounds of caramel each. But I'm going to need bigger ones if I'm going to export my caramels," he said.

Frank shook his head. "I don't know what to do. Let me think on your situation overnight. Come and see me at the bank in the morning." With that, the banker made his way out of the building.

Milton waited anxiously until the next morning. He felt that his entire future as a caramel maker in Lancaster depended on Frank's decision.

"I commend you on your honesty," Frank began. "I've spent a great deal of time pacing the floor and debating what to do about your outstanding loan and your request for another one." Milton held his breath. "And I have decided to take a chance on you, Mr. Hershey. However, I'm not sure that the bank manager would agree with my decision, so I am going to put the loan in my name. That way it won't raise any questions."

Milton was astonished. "Thank you!" he exclaimed. "I won't betray your trust. I'll get the English order filled quickly and be back with the money to repay the loan before it's due. I promise. You won't regret trusting me, Mr. Brenneman." He reached out and vigorously shook the banker's hand.

Minutes later, Milton left Lancaster National Bank with one thousand dollars in his pocket and big plans for the future. But first he had caramels to make—lots of them!

Milton was able to take over more space in the building and hire extra people to help make caramels. The group worked day and night. When they had finished, the caramels were packed into crates and sent off to New York City to be shipped to London. Now all Milton could do was wait, and waiting was hard for him. Doubt crept into his mind. What if the caramels were stored near the ship's boiler and got hot enough to spoil? What if Andrew Decies was not a man of his word or accepted the caramels but took his time sending payment to Milton? Milton could do nothing but hope that things went well.

On the Monday of the week the loan was due to be repaid, Milton had not heard from England. Tuesday came, and he nervously emptied his mailbox. Inside was a letter with a British postmark on it. Milton's hands shook as he opened the envelope. Inside was a check for five hundred British pounds—more than enough to pay off the loans when converted to US dollars—plus an order for even more caramels!

Milton let out a whoop of joy and grabbed his overcoat and hat. He ran down the street, laughing as he went. About halfway to the bank he realized he was still wearing his apron, speckled with sticky blobs of caramel. He tucked the apron into his belt and buttoned his coat as he ran. Breathless, Milton walked into the bank and straight over to Frank Brenneman. "I want my note, please. I've come to pay it off," he said.

Frank looked just as pleased as Milton felt. "Wonderful news, Mr. Hershey!" He eagerly took the check Milton handed to him.

It was a wonderful moment. Milton knew that all his hard work and the faith his mother, Aunt Mattie, and others had placed in him were at last paying off. He was debt free and, as far as he was concerned, on his way to making his dreams come true.

And so he was. Over the next six years Milton Hershey and the Lancaster Caramel Company grew quickly. True to his word, Andrew Decies kept placing large orders for caramels, and the profits from these shipments allowed Milton to expand his production and sales in the United States as well as experiment with all sorts of new shapes and flavors. While Milton did not fully understand the science behind candy making, he knew how to experiment with different textures, temperatures, and ingredients. He loved inventing new products and giving them catchy names. As the years rolled by, deluxe caramels made with Pennsylvania's best cream were named Lotus, Cocoanut Ices, and Paradox. Uniques, Melbas, and Empires were budget caramels made from skim milk and sold eight for a penny.

As his Crystal A Caramels grew more popular, Milton decided to expand his business. He invited Lebbie to work for him, and Lebbie did a good job managing the firm's financial records. Meanwhile, the brewery, the carriage-making shop, the carpet-beating business, and the piano and organ manufacturer moved out of the building. Milton took over their space until he occupied the entire building. Finally, he purchased the place and had two more stories added to facilitate increased caramel production.

Not long after this, he purchased several other buildings in Lancaster to serve as production facilities. When orders outpaced production at these facilities, Milton looked for others. Northwest of Lancaster at Mount Joy, he found a woolen-manufacturing plant. Milton bought the building, had the textile manufacturing equipment removed, and installed huge kettles and caramel-making equipment. Given his earlier business failure in New York City, Milton was pleased to be expanding his business operations again. To help stop transportation costs cutting into profits, Milton established a production facility in Chicago. This was a huge factory that occupied a seven-story building and employed four hundred workers. Milton asked his cousin Frank to run the plant. He called it the Western Branch, and he saw it as a hub, shipping caramels out to the spokes— other Midwest cities.

Still, there was not enough production capacity, and Milton started yet another factory, in Reading, Pennsylvania. Amazingly, people from all over the world were hearing about the caramels made by the Lancaster Caramel Company, and orders came in from as far as Australia, Japan, and China. It wasn't long before Milton's factories were working around the clock, churning out thousands of pounds of caramels a day.

All the while Milton's mother and Aunt Mattie insisted on continuing to play their role wrapping caramels, though Milton hardly needed their services. By 1893 he employed eight hundred people in Lancaster alone and another seven hundred in his other factories. His company was generating a million dollars' worth of business a year.

Milton could scarcely believe how wealthy he had become. When he started his business and sold caramels from a pushcart in the streets, many in Lancaster looked down on him. Now he was one of the city's most successful businessmen. And if he needed financing to expand his growing business, the banks were eager to lend him money. It had been an astonishing turnaround.

Milton bought himself a large house with a wide veranda wrapped around the front at 222 Queen Street in Lancaster. He had the house painted bright yellow and white. The place was surrounded by beautiful gardens that featured bright flowers and lively songbirds. Milton's mother lived with him at the house, and Milton was glad that she would never have to scrape by again.

Milton did not forget Aunt Mattie. He was grateful for all the support and advice she had given him over the years, and he bought her a house in Lancaster and paid for anything she needed.

By the beginning of 1893, everything in Milton Hershey's life was running smoothly. As the year progressed, he became interested in the World's Columbian Exposition that was slated to open in Chicago, commemorating the four-hundred-year anniversary of Christopher Columbus sailing from Europe to the New World. Milton thought back to the Centennial International Exhibition in Philadelphia seventeen years before. He had enjoyed the time he spent at that exhibition and the many interesting scientific and industrial breakthroughs he saw. So he decided to attend the upcoming exhibition in Chicago. Besides, Milton told himself, he could check up on his cousin Frank, who was running the new caramel factory in Chicago.

The World's Columbian Exposition opened on May 1, 1893. By the time Milton arrived in Chicago, several million people had already attended it. From the moment he stepped through the gates of the exhibition, Milton was impressed. The Centennial

International Exhibition in Philadelphia in 1876 had been a stunning affair, but this show outshined it. The exposition covered more than six hundred acres and consisted of nearly two hundred buildings built mostly in a neoclassical architectural style.

The buildings were covered in a stucco finish that was painted white and seemed to shine in the clear summer sun. At night, lit by electric lights, the buildings glowed. Milton could see why the exhibition area, set not far from the shore of nearby Lake Michigan, was being referred to as the White City.

Canals ran through the complex, and exhibition buildings were located around a lagoon, across which electric-powered boats ferried people. It wasn't just the buildings that impressed Milton. The gardens and lawns that surrounded them were immaculate. Not one blade of grass seemed to be out of place.

Inside the exhibit halls, all the wonders the world had to offer were on display. At the Centennial International Exhibition in Philadelphia, Milton had marveled at the latest in steam-engine technology, but in Chicago electricity took center stage. Not only was the whole exhibition site illuminated by electric lights, but also all sorts of electrical appliances and devices were on display. There was the first fully electrical kitchen, including an automatic dishwasher; a new form of phosphorescent lamps; and powerful electric motors that were fast replacing steam engines.

And there was the Ferris wheel. This huge metal wheel was 264 feet high and had thirty-six passenger cars that could accommodate sixty people each.

Once the passenger cars were loaded, the wheel rotated, giving the passengers in each car a bird's-eye view of the exhibition when their car reached the apex of the turning wheel.

One of the exhibit halls that Milton particularly liked was Agriculture Hall. The outside of the building was spectacular, with its high columns and a roof topped with a statue of the Greek goddess Diana. It was the inside of the building, however, that made Milton's heart race. It was where the latest food-related exhibits from forty-six countries around the world were housed. The United States had several interesting new foods on display: Shredded Wheat, Coca-Cola, Pillsbury flour, Lipton tea, Juicy Fruit chewing gum, and a new, convenient way to eat a meal—the hamburger.

As Milton made his way around the exhibits in Agriculture Hall, he came upon a display by a German company named Gebrueder Stollwerck, from the city of Cologne. The company made chocolate. To advertise their wares, the Stollwerck brothers had erected a thirty-eight-foot-tall temple made of thirty-thousand pounds of chocolate supported by a wooden frame. In the center of the chocolate temple was a ten-foot-high statue of Germania—the symbol of the Stollwerck chocolate company—also made entirely of chocolate.

Another chocolate display at the exhibition impressed Milton even more. This display was located in the Palace of Mechanical Arts and was not so much a display as it was a working factory. The J. M. Lehmann Company of Dresden, Germany, had set up an entire chocolate-manufacturing plant in the exhibit hall. Everything about the exhibit fascinated Milton, who watched carefully as the cocoa beans were shoveled into an oven to be roasted. Then the beans were cooled with blowers and hulled in a special machine. The chocolate nibs were ground to produce a thick liquid called chocolate liquor, which consisted of cocoa solids suspended in cocoa butter. Some of the chocolate liquor was squeezed to extract the cocoa butter, while the rest was poured into large pans containing marble rollers. Hour after hour, the liquor went back and forth as the marble rollers smoothed out its consistency. Then the rich, brown mixture was poured into presses to remove excess moisture before cocoa butter, sugar, and vanilla were added and the resulting chocolate concoction was poured into molds. Once the chocolate had cooled, it was tipped out of the molds and wrapped. When Milton tried a sample of the Lehmann chocolate, he realized that he had never tasted anything like it before. It was creamy and smooth, unlike gritty American chocolate.

While in Chicago, Milton visited a place that was not part of the World's Columbian Exposition—Pullman, Illinois. This was a new town of twelve thousand residents, built to house railroad-car manufacturer George Pullman's factory workers. It featured neat rows of brick houses, each with internal plumbing and gas. The town also had a large commercial arcade, churches, and other amenities, such as a library and parks. As Milton walked the streets of Pullman, he was most impressed with the place. The town was modern and clean and seemed to be a nice place to live.

Despite all the other attractions, Milton was continually drawn back to the J. M. Lehmann Company's chocolate exhibit in the Palace of Mechanical Arts. Not only did Milton find the smell of the chocolate intoxicating, but he was also fascinated by the whole process of producing the product. Milton visited the exhibit so many times that he got to know the people running the chocolate factory. On one visit Milton turned to his cousin Frank and said, "You mark my words, Frank. The caramel business is a fad. Chocolate will be a permanent thing." Milton had a new plan formulating in his head.

Chapter 10

A Million Dollars

We might have to get the floor reinforced. How much did that man say a mixer weighs?" Milton asked.

Frank frowned. "I think he said they weigh ten tons apiece. I didn't think about the flooring."

"No matter, we'll make it work," Milton responded.

It was October 30, 1893, closing day of the World's Columbian Exposition in Chicago. Milton was confident that his team could find their way around any obstacles associated with buying J. M. Lehmann Company's chocolate-making machinery. Milton had just paid twenty thousand dollars for the actual machinery that had been on display at the exhibition. He had watched this machinery at work so many times he decided it was better to purchase it rather than have a new set of machines shipped from Germany. Milton also hired Gerhard Wunderlich, the German mechanic responsible for keeping the machines running during the exhibition. Gerhard would move to Lancaster to help set up and run the machinery there.

"This is the future. I'm sure of it, Frank," Milton said to his cousin. "The more I study the numbers, the better I feel about this. Ten years ago the United States imported nine million pounds of cocoa beans, and this year we're on track to import twenty-four million pounds. Chocolate is going to get bigger and bigger in this country, and my new equipment can turn out five thousand pounds of it a day. I can't wait to get started."

Frank nodded. "The only thing I worry about is exactly how to make chocolate. You'll have the machinery, but no one is willing to share the exact recipe for making the chocolate."

Milton smiled. "That shouldn't be a problem once we get everything set up. I have the general idea. How hard can it be to find just the right balance?"

Sadly for Milton, it turned out to be a lot harder than he had imagined. The chocolate-making equipment was set up in an out-of-the-way corner on the third floor of the Lancaster Caramel Company's main building in Lancaster. Milton spent hundreds of hours trying to make tasteful chocolate. The problem was that there were so many variables involved in the process. The roasting of the cocoa beans, hulling them, grinding the nibs to make chocolate liquor, squeezing it to get cocoa butter, mixing the chocolate liquor to smooth it out, adding the right quantity of cocoa butter, sugar, and vanilla to the mixture— all were very complex steps in the chocolate-making process, more complex than Milton had thought. Nonetheless, he worked hard at trying to solve the chocolate puzzle.

Almost every day his mother and Aunt Mattie would come by the factory to encourage Milton, who was grateful for their belief in his schemes. It was particularly difficult and sad for Milton when, on April 10, 1894, Aunt Mattie died. She had been ill for only a few days, and her death came as a shock to Milton, his mother, and the Snavely clan.

Milton arranged a funeral for his aunt and even managed to persuade the conservative Mennonite pastor to fill the church with flowers, something that went against Mennonite tradition. Milton loved flowers and wanted some way to show how much Martha "Mattie" Snavely had meant to him.

As he sat in the front pew of the church during the funeral service, Milton thought back on all the times that Aunt Mattie had loaned him money and all the times she had patted him on the back and said, "Milt, keep going. Don't give up. God doesn't honor quitters." This had been good advice, and Milton was glad that his aunt had lived long enough to know that the faith she had put in her nephew was justified. He had been happy that in recent years he had seen to it that Aunt Mattie and his mother had everything they needed. Aunt Mattie's death left a hole in Milton's life, but he knew he had to go on. More challenges awaited—challenges Aunt Mattie would have urged him to overcome.

A year after purchasing the chocolate-making equipment from the J. M. Lehmann Company, long past the time when Milton had expected to be manufacturing chocolate, he was still trying to perfect the recipe. He tried a different tack and hired two chocolate makers from a factory in Switzerland. The plan worked, and it was not long before delicious chocolate was flowing into the molds to set. Now Milton had something he could work with.

Milton's imagination worked overtime as he came up with 114 ways to use the chocolate he was now making. He coated caramels with it, made various shaped chocolates, and sold tins of cocoa powder under the brand name Hershey Cocoa. Each of the chocolate product lines Milton produced had a creative name such as Smart Set, Opera, or Hero of Manila (a reference to the American capture of the Philippines during the Spanish-American War).

Once Milton had solved the problem of how to make chocolate with his new German equipment, he turned his attention to another challenge: what to do with his father. Milton and his father had kept in touch by letters through the years, and Milton had sent him money to live on. But now, in 1896, Henry was sixty-seven years old, too old in Milton's opinion to be living out West on his own. Milton developed an elaborate plan to bring his father home and hopefully reunite his parents.

The first step in the plan involved buying the Hershey family farm and homestead at Derry Church.
This was the farm where Milton and his father had
both been born. But when Milton's grandfather died
years before, the farm was sold. Now it was time to
buy it back. Milton did not care how much it cost.
He could afford whatever price the current owner
wanted. As it turned out, it cost Milton ten thousand
dollars to buy back the farm with its large two-story
house and wide veranda, a barn and several out-
buildings, and forty acres of land.

In January 1897 Milton visited the Hershey farm
and homestead he now owned. The old home was
more run-down that he had imagined it would be,
and he made arrangements to have the place repaired
and painted. He also asked Lebbie to move into the
house to supervise the work. When the house had
been fixed up, Milton wrote to his father and invited
him to take up residence at the old family farm.

Henry arrived back at Derry Church with the
usual fanfare that followed him wherever he went.
He wore a silk suit and carried a gold-tipped cane
and informed Milton that his last scheme had been
running a used book store in Denver. He added that
since he could not imagine dumping the wonderful
array of books he had in inventory in the store, he
had packed them up and brought them all with him.
(He quietly asked Milton if he would pay the freight
cost required to get them from Colorado to Pennsylvania.) There were enough books to fill a bookcase
twelve feet long and seven feet high. Milton seldom

read a book himself, but he smiled when he saw all his father's books. His mother did not. "Too much reading will be the death of him," she grumbled. "If he had worked as much as he read, we wouldn't have been dirt poor when we were married."

Milton winced at his mother's words. He did not think it wise to point out to her that they still were married, even though for many years she had registered herself as a widow at church. She did not take well to the idea of having her colorful husband back in the district. Her reaction made Milton see that it was unrealistic to think his parents would ever get back together, but he was happy to have his father's company again and to know that his father was now well taken care of.

Soon after Henry arrived at Derry Church, his sister, Elizabeth, who could be just as stubborn as her older brother, needed a place to live. She also moved into the old Hershey homestead. Lebbie, Henry, and Elizabeth made for an odd assortment of people, and there was always something interesting happening at the farm.

With his family as settled as they were ever likely to be, Milton's life took a turn he never expected. At thirty-nine years of age, he fell madly in love. He had not bothered to date women before. He always had too much to do with his business. But now a young woman, twenty-six-year-old Catherine Sweeney, had captured his heart.

Milton met Catherine, or Kitty, as everyone called her, while on a business trip to Jamestown, New York. He was visiting a candy store there when he noticed her. Milton was immediately smitten—Kitty was a beautiful young woman with auburn hair and flashing brown eyes. He wondered how his life would change if he pursued her. Would he make a good husband? Was he too old to raise children of his own? How would his mother react if he brought home a young Irish Catholic woman?

Soon after they met, Catherine moved to New York City, where she got a job at the ribbon counter at Altman's Department Store. Before he knew it, Milton was making up excuses to go to New York almost every weekend. He took Kitty to restaurants, the opera, plays, and Coney Island, where they loved to walk along the boardwalk together. A year after they met, Milton asked Kitty to marry him.

Milton and Catherine were married on May 25, 1898, in the rectory at St. Patrick's Cathedral on Fifth Avenue in New York. No one was there to witness the event. Milton traveled with Kitty back to Lancaster to introduce her to his mother.

Fanny Hershey was not impressed with her new daughter-in-law. Kitty was vivacious and witty. She loved to play the piano and sing, two pursuits that Milton's Mennonite mother found frivolous. Milton soon realized that it was not going to be a happy home with the three of them living under one roof, and he bought his mother a home of her own.

Milton doted on Kitty, who shared his love of flowers. Every day he ordered fresh flowers to be placed on her nightstand. Many times he even picked the flowers himself. He also had some portrait photographs taken of his new wife, and when he had to go away on business trips, he always packed a photo of Kitty in his bag.

On those business trips, Milton often thought about caramels and chocolate. He knew that the American public's demand for caramels was tapering off and their demand for chocolates was rising. He had a hunch that this trend would become more pronounced as the century ended, that chocolate was the future and caramels the past.

During 1898 the owners of Milton's rival, the American Caramel Company, approached him and asked whether he would be willing to merge his caramel company with theirs. They pointed out that if the two companies were combined, they would control 95 percent of caramel sales in the United States. While this was true, Milton was not interested in linking the two companies. He did not want the problems that went along with such mergers. Besides, he was ready to get out of the caramel business. Milton declined the offer and waited.

As he thought might happen, the American Caramel Company subsequently offered to buy the Lancaster Caramel Company outright. Now Milton felt there was something to talk about. He ordered his lawyer, John Snyder, to negotiate for the highest price possible for the company and to make it clear to the American Caramel Company that he was selling only his caramel business, which included production facilities and machinery and the rights to all trademarked caramel brands. Milton was going to keep the chocolate production side of his business, including the Hershey Cocoa brand name, the chocolate manufacturing equipment, and the current chocolate products he made and sold.

As the negotiations to sell his company dragged on, Milton traveled with Kitty to New York. A new technological phenomenon—the motorcar, or horseless carriage, as it was being called—was beginning to capture the imagination of the American public. In February 1900 the first major automobile show in the United States was to be held at Madison Square Garden, and Milton attended it. He was fascinated by this new invention and wanted to learn all he could about motorcars.

Milton was impressed by what he saw at the show. Most of the cars truly did look like horseless carriages, and it was a little disconcerting at first to see one making its way along the street without a horse pulling it. What really impressed Milton was a demonstration of a vehicle made by the Riker Electric Vehicle Company that drove off a platform and down a ramp onto the show floor. Milton realized that even a regular buggy, without a horse attached, would roll down an incline like that. What really caught his attention was when the vehicle braked, turned around, and accelerated back up the ramp onto the platform.

Following the demonstration, Milton sought out the Riker Electric Vehicle exhibit to learn more. At the exhibit he spotted one of the company's vehicles with a delivery van body on it. He watched as a driver demonstrated the vehicle for him, steering it with a brass lever on the left side. Milton learned that the delivery van was powered by a battery that could store enough electricity for the van to cover thirty miles at a top speed of nine miles per hour. Milton was impressed, so impressed that he bought the delivery van from the car show floor for two thousand dollars, with orders that it be delivered to Lancaster.

Lancaster had no motorcars. Milton decided that the Riker delivery van would be a wonderful advertisement as it drove around town delivering Hershey Cocoa to stores. The vehicle was painted black, with "Hershey Cocoa" painted on each side. Milton hired a man to drive the new contraption. Wherever the Riker traveled around town, a crowd gathered to watch. Milton hoped these crowds would buy some of the cocoa the van was delivering.

Meanwhile, it took many months of haggling between the lawyers for each of the caramel companies, but eventually an amount that the American Caramel Company would pay to buy the Lancaster Caramel Company was agreed upon. Milton signed the papers to sell his company, and the August 10, 1900, edition of *The Philadelphia Inquirer* carried the headline: "CARAMEL FACTORY SOLD; MILTON S. HERSHEY RECEIVES A MILLION DOLLARS FOR IT."

Fourteen years had passed since Milton had returned to Lancaster from his failed candy business in New York. In the intervening years, Milton had built a successful business worth a million dollars. He wished that Aunt Mattie could have been around to see the day.

Milton was now forty-two years old, still young enough to enjoy himself. He had a beautiful wife, all the money he could ever ask for, and his two parents living close by. He was a happy man.

While Milton intended to develop his chocolate business, for the time being he was content to let things roll along. As part of the sale of the Lancaster Caramel Company, he had negotiated to rent the space in the main factory building that housed his chocolate-manufacturing equipment. Milton asked William Murrie, who had been his sales manager for the caramel company, to run the chocolate business while he took a break. Kitty had been in ill health recently, and Milton thought that a trip to Europe and Egypt would be good for them both. It would also give Kitty the opportunity to seek medical treatment from European specialists and find answers to improving her health.

Chapter 11

The Challenge of Milk Chocolate

Six months after Milton was handed the check for one million dollars for the Lancaster Caramel Company, he would gladly have swapped it for one piece of good news from Dr. Wilhelm Erb in Germany. From the time they were married, Kitty had experienced times when she felt weak and on occasion had even collapsed. Doctors in the United States could not diagnose what was wrong with her, and so while Milton and Kitty were traveling in Europe, they went to see more doctors. Although they found one who understood Kitty's illness, the doctor's diagnosis was anything but comforting.

Dr. Erb told the couple that Kitty had an incurable condition affecting her nerves. He went on to predict that some days she would feel fine and on other days she would be bedridden. She would also eventually become a cripple and most likely would die young. This was devastating news for Milton and Kitty. Nothing meant more to Milton than the happiness of his wife, and now it seemed that they might not have a long life together.

Milton tried hard to do everything he could to cheer Kitty up. He bought her expensive jewelry and hats with huge plumes. The couple traveled to Paris to attend the theater, one of Kitty's favorite activities, and eat at fine Parisian restaurants. But somehow all of these activities did not bring as much joy as Milton thought they would.

Milton and Kitty traveled on to Egypt to see the Great Pyramids. Milton even rode on a camel. It was also in Egypt that Milton had to face his future. One day he sat staring silently out the window of his Cairo hotel, the outline of the pyramids silhouetted against the horizon, date palms swaying in the breeze.

"Are you all right?" Kitty asked. "You look distracted."

Milton turned over the box of Nestlé milk chocolate in his hands. "I'm just thinking."

"About milk chocolate?" Kitty inquired.

"Yes, about milk chocolate."

"Milton," Kitty said as she sat down beside him, "you've talked about milk chocolate so much during this trip, are you sure you wouldn't be happier back in Lancaster trying to work out the recipe for it yourself?"

"But we don't need the money. We have more money than we could ever spend."

"I know," Kitty sighed. "It's never really been about the money with you, though, has it? It's about the challenge, about putting your apron on and getting down to work. I don't think you were cut out to spend the rest of your days living the life of a retired gentleman."

"But what about your illness? The best doctors are in Germany. Don't you think we should stay close to them?"

Kitty shook her head. "There's nothing the doctors in Europe can do for me that I couldn't do in Lancaster. I can hire a nurse and have her trained to massage my legs, and I'm sure all the medicines Dr. Erb recommends are available in the United States. Let's go home."

Milton put his hand on Kitty's knee and looked into her brown eyes. "You know, I think you're quite right, my dear. I'm happiest when I have something to do." He lifted up the box of milk chocolate. "I'm sure I can figure out how to make this. And then I'll work out how to make it cheaply so that everyone in America can afford good milk chocolate. Why, I think I'll start making five-cent bars of chocolate—Hershey bars. They'll be for sale at every cinema, drugstore counter, and bowling alley in the country."

"Look at you!" Kitty smiled. "Your eyes are shining. That's more like the man I married."

Milton laughed. It felt good to think about going home again.

When Milton and Kitty arrived back in Lancaster, people were glad to see that they had returned early. Milton was delighted to learn that his chocolate-manufacturing business was thriving under William Murrie's able direction.

After settling back into the house on South Queen Street, Milton set to work on unraveling the secret of milk chocolate. During his time in Europe, he had learned a few things about the process. He knew that the Swiss used milk powder to make their milk chocolate, while the English used condensed milk. But on the voyage home from Europe, Milton had thought a lot about the process, and he had a different idea.

Milton rolled up his sleeves and started his experiments. He soon discovered that mixing milk and chocolate together was very difficult. Milk is nearly 90 percent water, and chocolate has a high proportion of cocoa butter—a fat—and the fat and water did not mix. The cocoa butter settled in globs on top of the milk. To make matters worse, the milk fat turned the chocolate rancid. Milton tried everything he could think of to combine the milk and chocolate, but nothing seemed to work.

Milton was conducting the experiments in the space his chocolate company rented from the American Caramel Company, but soon he decided that he needed more space and privacy to continue his experiments. He knew just where to go to find that space and privacy—the old Hershey farm in Derry Church. Milton had a creamery and a small chocolate factory built behind the old family homestead, and the buildings were fitted with the latest equipment. When his experimental facility was complete, Milton moved into the homestead so he could save time by not having to commute from Lancaster each day. Kitty continued to live at the house in Lancaster and would visit Milton often.

Now Milton was ready to solve the mystery of making good milk chocolate. He decided to start at the beginning, with the cows that made the milk and the grass the cows ate. He wanted to know how the kind of grass a cow ate affected her milk. He also wanted to know which breed of cows produced the most suitable milk for chocolate. He started with a herd of forty-eight Jersey cows.

Milton hired several young men to help him with his experiments and went to work. Life soon fell into a busy routine for him and his helpers. Milton would be up at 4:30 each morning to milk the cows. Following the milking, he would eat breakfast and then head to the creamery to process the fresh milk. The cows would have to be milked again at the end of the day.

Fanny insisted on moving out to the farm to supervise the housework and cooking. She chose a bedroom as far as possible from Milton's father. Despite the fact that his parents lived at opposite ends of the house, Milton was grateful that they were at least living under the same roof again.

By now Milton realized that he needed to condense the milk he was using to reduce the amount of water it contained. This was done by heating the milk for a long time to evaporate the water. Since

Milton assumed that the richest milk would make the best milk chocolate, he started using cream. He soon found out that this approach would not work. The cream burned during the process and had to be dumped and the kettles cleaned. He switched to using whole milk. This worked better, but the process was still tricky. Then Milton encountered another problem: when he added sugar to the condensed milk, the ingredients did not blend properly. So he began adding the sugar at the start of the condensing process. This worked better and caused more water to be evaporated from the mixture.

Weeks turned into months, and still Milton had not solved the riddle of how to produce milk chocolate. Sometimes he would work through the night trying different approaches, locked away in his creamery with a sign on the door that read "No Admittance." His experiments often ended in failure and had to be dumped. It was frustrating, and Milton wished the whole process were simpler. Many variables needed to be taken into consideration, and at times the whole enterprise seemed overwhelming. Despite the frustrations and disappointments, Milton kept a positive attitude most of the time. He knew that if he kept on trying, he would eventually find the secret to making good milk chocolate. He was also driven by the fact that the first company to bring good milk chocolate to the American public stood to make a fortune.

The pressure on Milton to succeed mounted when he learned that Walter Baker and Company, a chocolate maker in Massachusetts, was also experimenting with milk chocolate. Given the difficulty of the challenge, Milton hoped he was farther ahead in his experiments than his competitor. He knew that whoever got his product into the marketplace first, at a good price, stood to win the lion's share of the milk chocolate market for years to come.

Milton continued his experiments month after month. He made breakthroughs and even managed to produce milk chocolate bars. The bars tasted sweet and had a smooth texture, but the chocolate turned rancid in a few days. This was not what Milton wanted. He wanted a milk chocolate bar that would stay fresh for months so that it could be shipped all over the United States. He experimented some more.

This time Milton decided to use skim instead of whole milk. He had separators installed in the creamery to separate the cream from the milk. Not wanting to waste the cream, he had it turned into high-quality butter, which he sold in Lancaster. Along with making the switch to skim milk, Milton decided to replace his herd of Jersey cows with Holsteins, which produced milk that contained far less fat than the milk from Jerseys.

Another kind of pressure began to bear down on Milton as he worked at his experiments. This time it was not pressure from a chocolate competitor but pressure from the success of his own chocolate business. The chocolate-manufacturing plant, still housed in rented space at the American Caramel Company in Lancaster, was turning out chocolate coatings for caramels, Hershey Cocoa powder, and a range of dark chocolate treats, or novelties, as they were referred to. Business was booming for these products, and as a result, they needed a bigger production space.

Milton wanted to build a large manufacturing facility equipped with modern European machinery. He just didn't know where to build it. At first he thought he would build the plant in Lancaster. He located a suitable plot of land near Franklin and Marshall College on the northwestern edge of Lancaster, but the land was too expensive. Milton also ran headlong into corrupt local politics. A prominent Lancaster political figure asked Milton for a large campaign contribution. When Milton refused, the politician informed him that he could expect to pay high taxes on any land he purchased in Lancaster.

Milton did not have time to play political games. He began to look elsewhere. Quietly he investigated possible sites in Baltimore, Maryland, and the New York City area, until an entire different line of thought struck him: why not build a new chocolate factory in Mennonite country? There were plenty of cows in the area to supply the necessary milk, along with a good supply of fresh water and strong, honest workmen to man the factory.

The more Milton thought about the concept, the more he liked it, especially the idea of building the new factory right on the edge of Derry Church. In March 1902 Milton set out to find just the right spot for a chocolate factory. On a cold, rainy day he donned a heavy overcoat and rubber boots and placed a floppy hat on his head before catching the train east to Palmyra, just a few miles away. As

Milton stared out the train window at the black-and-white cows grazing in pastures in the rain, he was sure he was making the right move.

In Palmyra, Milton headed for the Washington Hotel and announced that he needed to hire a horse and wagon and driver. A man named Moyer offered his services, and soon Milton was sitting on the wagon beside him as they made their way down a rutted road that headed west toward Hummelstown. As the wagon bumped along, Milton carefully studied the land along either side of the road. Most of it was divided into small family farms of up to about one hundred acres. These farms were at the bottom of the Lebanon Valley, where the land was rockier, not as fertile as that of the rolling green hills that surrounded the valley. Some of the farms were quite run-down, and Milton knew why. Because of advances in transportation and the preserving and packaging of food in the United States, farm produce was now being shipped from productive areas of the country to less productive areas and to the cities. This made it hard for local farmers to compete, especially those whose farms were located on less fertile land, such as those at the bottom of the Lebanon Valley. Yet although the farms were run-down and struggling, the land they occupied was perfect for Milton's needs.

As the day rolled on, the wagon driver tried to make conversation and inquire about Milton's plans. Milton told him nothing, not even his name. He simply told the wagon driver that he had been born in the area and wanted to see it again. Milton did not yet want anyone to know what he was up to for fear the price of the land would rise if news got out that a millionaire was looking to buy it.

When they reached a point near Derry Church where the spring that fed the local stream was located, Milton asked the driver to stop. He climbed off the wagon, clambered over a fence, and made his way through the long, wet grass to explore. Not too far from the clear spring water that bubbled out of the ground, Milton discovered a limestone cliff. "Perfect," he thought to himself. The limestone could be quarried and used as building material.

When they got back to Palmyra, Milton paid the driver and caught the train back to Derry Church. By the time he arrived at the Hershey homestead, he had made up his mind. There was plenty of good land on the edge of Derry Church, an abundant supply of clean water from the spring, and limestone that could be used for building. He would build the new Hershey chocolate factory at Derry Church. He had just one problem: a factory of the size he imagined would need workers, and those workers and their families would need a town to live in. Milton considered an idea as to how to solve that problem.

Chapter 12

"I'm Not Crazy"

I t will have everything a well-designed town needs,"
Milton told his cousin Bill Blair, manager of the
American Caramel Company's Lancaster factory. "A
swimming pool, theaters, banks, parks, golf courses,
libraries—it will all be there. I want to prove that giving people a wholesome place to live makes for good
citizens and a stable workforce." Milton paused,
waiting for his cousin's response. None came. "Don't
you have an opinion, Bill?" he asked.

Bill shook his head. "Do you *really* want my
opinion?"

"Of course I do."

"Then here it is, Milton. My opinion is that your
friends should go to court and have a guardian
appointed for you."

"But I'm not crazy," Milton replied. "Look, this all
makes perfect sense. Why try to compete for a labor

force when I can create my own town and house them all right there in the Lebanon Valley?"

"Alright," Bill said. "Assuming you go ahead with this, what are you going to do about getting gas and electricity and telephone lines to the town? Or train tracks? With so many things to think about, how are you going to concentrate on making chocolate?"

Milton stared at his cousin. Sometimes it was hard to find anyone who believed in his vision. "Those are small things," he replied. "I'm thinking of the big picture, a multimillion-dollar-a-year chocolate business that can and will support a healthy, clean, happy town. I'm going to do it, you'll see. Everything will fall into place."

Milton set to work planning his dream town on the edge of Derry Church. The first piece of the puzzle was to secure the land he needed to move ahead with the project. Milton hired Christian Maulfair, a local real estate agent, to obtain options to buy the land from the owners of the farms Milton had secretly inspected several weeks before. It wasn't long before Christian had secured options to buy twelve hundred acres of land at Derry Church for a cost of less than two hundred thousand dollars. The parcels of land under option included the limestone cliff Milton had discovered and the spring that Spring Creek flowed from. This was important to Milton, as the limestone would be used as a building material for the new chocolate factory and the spring would supply the clean water the factory would need.

In January 1903 Milton visited the office of Henry Herr, a civil engineer in Lancaster. He described his vision for the new factory and town he wanted to build thirty miles away at Derry Church. He explained that he wanted to hire the civil engineer to survey the land and lay out a plan on the land under option. At first Henry's reaction was similar to that of Milton's cousin Bill. The engineer had never even heard of Derry Church and explained that no one had ever proposed doing what Milton proposed. New factories were built close to cities, where there was an adequate supply of workers and good transportation links. At Derry Church there was neither. But when he realized that Milton was serious about his plan, Henry agreed to survey the land and draw up a master plan for the new factory and town.

A short time afterward, Henry had a band of surveyors secretly surveying four thousand acres of land at Derry Church. Henry had explained to Milton that they needed to do this in order to draw up a detailed contour map of the area that would show every five-foot change in elevation as well as every rocky outcrop, creek bed, and hill. The map would give the civil engineer a clearer picture of Milton's optioned twelve hundred acres of land in relation to the surrounding countryside and would guide him as he sited the new factory and town on that land.

Once the survey was complete and the map produced, Henry chose a site for the new chocolate factory. He began laying out the site plan for Milton's new town, along with the trolley car line Milton intended to build from Campbelltown through his new town to Hummelstown. The trolley cars would be able to ferry future workers who did not choose to live in the town to and from the chocolate factory. When the proposed street grid for the new town was finalized, Milton named the two main streets Cocoa and Chocolate Avenues. The cross streets were named after the various places from which he imported his cacao beans: Ceylon, Caracas, Java, Granada, and Areba.

Although Milton had hoped to keep his plans as secret as possible, in February 1903, as Henry drew up site plans for the new factory and town, word leaked out. The newspaper headline told of Milton Hershey's plans to build a "chocolate town."

Once the site plan for the town was established, Milton hired a Lancaster architect named Emlen Urban to design his new chocolate factory and the public buildings for the town. On the highest point overlooking the new factory and town, Milton planned to build a grand house for himself and Kitty.

The factory Milton intended to build would be the most modern chocolate factory in the world. It would be 700 feet long and 350 feet wide and cover nearly six acres of land. In fact, what he envisioned was eighteen separate single-story buildings connected by long corridors. At each end of the factory would be a railway spur connecting to the main line between Harrisburg and Philadelphia. Boxcar loads of cacao beans would arrive at one end of the factory. The beans would be roasted in ovens and then moved on to the next part of the factory, where the husks would be removed and the nibs separated. The nibs would then be ground to make chocolate liquor before going on to the next step in the manufacturing process. Chocolate bars would then arrive at the other end of the factory, where they would be wrapped and packed into boxes and loaded into boxcars to be shipped across the United States.

While Emlen Urban designed the new chocolate factory and civic building for the town, Milton began buying up the twelve hundred acres of land. Soon afterward, in the spring, fifty workers began clearing the land where the factory was to be built, using dynamite to reach the bedrock on which to lay a foundation. Milton watched with excitement as construction of his new chocolate factory and town began.

With foundation work under way, Milton turned his attention back to something just as important. He still did not know the secret to making large quantities of long-lasting, quality milk chocolate. He tried not to let this concern him, but the fact was, the new factory and town could flourish only if Milton determined how to make good, cheap milk chocolate to sell to the masses. The pressure was on him to come up with the secret, and soon.

Milton had traded out the large open kettle in his experimental facility at the Hershey homestead for a long, panlike, sealed copper kettle in which to boil the milk in the condensing process. This new kettle allowed the milk to be boiled in a vacuum and the water to be sucked away as it vaporized from the milk solids. Milton was sure that adding the sugar to the milk before it was boiled and condensed was the right sequence, but it seemed almost impossible to boil the milk down without scalding it on the bottom of the pan, creating a burnt, sticky mess.

While Milton toiled away trying to unlock the secret of making milk chocolate, the new factory began to take shape. A crew of men were busy quarrying the limestone from the cliff, and stonemasons were building the factory walls. Work also started on the brick smokestack that would rise to a height of 150 feet. The smokestack would vent smoke from the power plant, where huge boilers would produce steam to turn dynamos that generated the electricity needed to power the new factory and town.

As the factory took shape, Milton began to fret about milk chocolate. What was the secret? What was he missing? Despite liking to work things out for himself, Milton finally decided to bring in an outside expert. He hired a chemist to work alongside him at the experimental factory and to advise him as to what he might be doing wrong. When the chemist burned the first batch of milk he tried to condense, Milton let him go. He then turned for help to John Schmalbach, a trusted and competent worker at Milton's chocolate plant in Lancaster.

John arrived at the Hershey homestead late in the afternoon. After eating dinner with Milton and his parents, the two men made their way to the creamery behind the house. First they had to scrape and clean the inside of the vacuum kettle after an earlier failed attempt. As they worked, Milton described the problem he was having. John didn't say much as he listened to what Milton had to say.

Once the kettle was cleaned, Milton and John poured fresh skim milk into it and added sugar.

Once the kettle was filled, John took command of the process. At first he didn't apply too much heat and just let the mixture warm through. Then he began to gradually increase the heat, gently cooking the milk and sugar mixture and allowing the water to evaporate. After several hours of cooking this way, John slowly brought the temperature down and let the mixture cool for a while. As John cooked the mixture, Milton took careful note of everything he did. If this approach was successful, he would be able to replicate it.

John's approach was successful. When the kettle was opened, inside was a perfect batch of smooth, sweet condensed milk. Milton was delighted. In all his attempts to produce condensed milk, he had never produced anything near the quality of the batch John had just made. Not only was it quality, but also it blended together easily with the chocolate liquor, cocoa butter, and other ingredients. Milton was overjoyed.

Milton sampled the blended mixture several days later, after it had been through the smoothing process and left to set. The milk chocolate melted in his mouth. The chocolate was sweet and smooth and had a slight sour taste to it that European milk chocolate did not have. Milton knew that Americans were going to love the taste of his milk chocolate. Not only was it creamy, sweet, and smooth, but he soon discovered that it stayed fresh for up to two months.

At last Milton had a recipe and procedure. Over the next months, he made many batches of milk chocolate, refining the process and working out how to scale it up for mass production in his new factory.

The new chocolate factory was coming together better than Milton could have imagined. The smokestack was complete, the factory walls were up, and the slate roof was in place. Carpenters, plasterers, plumbers, and electricians were now busy inside the building, often working late into the night preparing the interior of the building and fitting it with new equipment Milton had ordered from Europe. Milton would often walk around the building site with his father. He loved the way his father's eyes shined when he noticed some recent innovation in the factory. Henry also was particularly impressed and delighted by the massive power-generating facility that was taking shape to provide the electricity to run the factory.

In early February 1904, Milton felt that things were enough under control for him to take Kitty on a trip to Florida. Kitty's health was continually up and down, and she found that the long northern winters drained her energy and made her bones ache. Milton felt that spending time in Florida would be good for his wife's health. They had been in Florida a few days when Milton received a telegram. His father had died of a heart attack. Milton could hardly believe it. His father had always seemed so fit and was constantly joking that he was as healthy as a horse and would live to be a hundred.

Milton made arrangements for him and Kitty to be on the next train north. Two days later, Milton and Kitty were back in Derry Church. On his arrival, Milton learned that his father had been visiting a relative, Dr. Martin Hershey, and upon leaving the doctor's house had decided to walk home in the snow. Evidently the exertion was too much for him, and he had collapsed outside the homestead. Two of Milton's assistants saw him collapse and carried him inside. Henry died on the couch a few minutes later.

Milton was devastated. He enjoyed his father's company and relied on him to bounce ideas off of. Henry always saw the possibilities and never the problems, and Milton would miss that the most. Milton's mother saw things differently. After the funeral, when Milton was back home in Lancaster with Kitty, Fanny persuaded one of the young workers at the experimental creamery to throw all of her dead husband's books into a wheelbarrow and, one barrow load at a time, take them to the furnace in the experimental facility, where she pitched them into the fire. Hours later, not a single book was left in Henry Hershey's library.

Milton was sad when he learned what his mother had done, but he understood. Fanny had always felt that Henry had been led astray by the strange ideas he read in books, and it was her way of having the last say.

Milton took a long time after his father's death to regain his enthusiasm for life. He often wished the old man was around to study building plans with him or help map out the route of the tracks for the railway spur that would soon be laid to the new factory. Like Milton, his father had always loved trains and railroads.

By the fall of 1904, individually designed houses were being built along the streets of the new town.

Milton had made it clear that he did not want his new town to be like any other company town where workers simply rented a house in a long row of houses that all looked identical. He had seen this approach at Pullman in Chicago when he visited during the 1893 World's Columbian Exposition. Milton wanted his workers to own their own uniquely designed houses and feel like they were living in a real town. He believed that in buying their homes, people were also taking ownership of the town. And if people bought their houses and raised their families in the town, this would lead to a stable workforce. When this advice was ignored and the first few houses built all looked the same, Milton ordered them torn down and individually unique houses to be built in their place. Not only were the houses to be individually designed, but also they were built with the best available materials and fitted with the latest amenities, such as indoor plumbing, central heating, and electricity.

In fall 1904 the trolley line from Campbelltown to Hummelstown was completed. Milton invited a group of twenty dignitaries from the surrounding towns and Lancaster on an inaugural trolley trip. Milton joined them as the trolley rolled smoothly along on the newly constructed line. When they reached the chocolate factory, the trolley stopped for a tour of the nearly completed facility. Milton started by showing the dignitaries the power-generating plant with its huge boilers and dynamos. Then he walked them through the factory from one end to the other, explaining each step in the chocolate-making

process as he went. The tour took them past workers busily installing the chocolate-making machinery that had just arrived from Europe.

At the end of the tour, Milton took the dignitaries
to the new office block, where they were all served
a meal. After dinner and a number of toasts to Milton's success, they all climbed back onto the trolley
and completed the trip to Hummelstown.

Milton could hardly wait to begin production. At
the facility in Lancaster he had produced a range of
chocolate novelties to sell. At the new factory he was
going to do things differently. He would no longer
produce the range of chocolate novelties but instead
focus on one thing: a five-cent milk-chocolate Hershey bar. He knew the new chocolate bar would be
a winner.

Chapter 13

Hershey, Pennsylvania

Milton picked another envelope from the pile and opened it. "'Etabit.' What do you think of that one, Kitty?"

Kitty smiled. "I hope people eat a lot, not a bit!" she quipped.

Milton laughed. "You're so right. So many names to choose from. How ever are we going to find the best one?"

The new town in the Derry Church pastureland was taking shape, and the Hershey Chocolate Company was sponsoring a competition to find a suitable name for it. The one-hundred-dollar prize being offered had inspired thousands of entries that included Ulikit, Cocoa-hirsh, Chococoa City, Majestic, Zenith, Oasis, and one that sent Kitty into giggles, St. Milton.

Eventually "Hersheykoko" was judged the winning entry. It had been sent in by Mrs. Doyle of Wilkes-Barre, Pennsylvania, who received the award. However, when Milton applied to the postmaster general to create a post office for the town, he was told that the name Hersheykoko sounded too commercial and a new post office would not be approved under that name. Milton went back to the entries and had an assistant select another one. Over two thousand people had entered the simple name "Hershey" for the town, and Milton decided that was good enough. The new name was submitted to the postmaster general and accepted, and soon a new post office was being constructed in Hershey, Pennsylvania. Milton was sad that his father was not around to enjoy the moment.

As 1905 rolled around, most of the new chocolate-making equipment from Europe had been installed in the factory, and Milton began to wind down production at his facility in Lancaster. Slowly over several months, the machinery was moved out of the rented space in the American Caramel Company's building and installed in the new factory at Hershey.

At the same time, workers began to move into their new homes. For many of them it was the first time they had ever lived in a new house equipped with internal plumbing, central heating, and electricity. Most people welcomed these new modern amenities, but a few had difficulty adjusting to electricity. Somehow electric lights scared them, and they chose to use kerosene lamps instead. It did not take them long, however, to discover the convenience of flicking a switch for lighting rather than having to prime and light a lamp. Soon the glow of electric lights could be seen from the windows of all the houses in town.

In June 1905 the new factory was ready to begin production. William Murrie, who had been running Milton's chocolate-manufacturing facility in Lancaster, was made operations manager. Soon boxcar loads of cacao beans began arriving, and the roasters were fired up. Milk from the surrounding dairy farms also flowed in. After the milk was separated into skim milk, the condensing process began in the new vacuum kettles. Chocolate liquor, cocoa butter, and other ingredients were added to the condensed milk, followed by four days of smoothing the mixture in conching machines. The chocolate was then sent to the molding department, where it was molded and set into chocolate bars. The bars were wrapped and boxed for shipping, and a week after beginning production, the first boxcar loaded with Hershey Milk Chocolate bars was ready to be shipped.

Now that his factory was mass producing Hershey bars, Milton sent sales representatives around the country to visit retailers and secure orders. Soon it seemed that Hershey bars were for sale everywhere.

By June 1906, net sales of Hershey chocolate had reached a million dollars. Milton was delighted and was sure it was only the beginning. It helped that he had no competition in the country selling milk chocolate. As he had predicted, the price of five cents a chocolate bar was irresistible to Americans, who fell in love with the taste of the new chocolate.

While the factory continued to mass produce Hershey bars and money kept rolling in to the company, there was still plenty to do in Hershey—and funds with which to do it. Milton bought more dairy farms around Hershey to keep up with the ever-increasing supply of milk the chocolate factory needed and started building more amenities in town. A modern school was built to replace the old Derry Church school, a department store was built on the corner of Cocoa and Chocolate Avenues, and a bank was set up. Soon an inn was erected. Milton also persuaded the owners of the Philadelphia & Reading Railroad, whose railway ran through town, to build a fancy new station to replace the old Derry Church station. Then Milton established a park that was free for all to use. The park contained a football field, a pavilion where dances were held, a refreshment stand, and an outdoor theater where touring vaudeville acts performed. Milton had plans to build a golf course and even a zoo for the town.

Milton and Kitty also broke ground on their new home to be called High Point, because it was set on a rocky outcrop overlooking the factory and town. The house was built of local stone and had four large columns that held up a high portico in front. Inside the front hallway a grand staircase ascended to the second floor, where the bedrooms were located. The house was big, but it was modest by the standards of other millionaires' mansions of the day, such as the massive and lavish chateau known as Biltmore that

George Vanderbilt had constructed a decade before near Asheville, North Carolina. Milton wanted no such place. He wanted a home where he and Kitty could be comfortable and where they had adequate room to entertain guests. In truth, even though he was now quite wealthy, Milton never strayed far from his Mennonite roots. He did not appreciate things that were showy and pretentious but preferred things to be modest and useful.

With the success of his Hershey bar, Milton developed several other milk chocolate products. The first was small, conical-shaped drops of chocolate individually wrapped in foil and sold in a box. Milton called these chocolate drops Sweethearts, which were introduced in 1907. Like the Hershey bar, the Sweethearts were a huge success, though Milton soon renamed the product Hershey Kisses. Soon after Hershey Kisses, a milk chocolate bar with almonds was introduced and also became a success. Sales of all three products steadily grew, with profits for the chocolate company more than doubling.

In the spring of 1908, Milton and Kitty moved into High Point. Like their previous house in Lancaster, the new place was surrounded by magnificent gardens filled with roses, chrysanthemums, tulips, hyacinths, and boxwood. Kitty spent much of her day overseeing the gardens and enjoying the view from the "bird's nest" Milton had built for her. This was a platform in a large spreading oak that had a gently sloping ramp up to it so that it was easily accessible for Kitty.

Later in the year, Milton felt things were running smoothly enough at the chocolate factory and town for him and Kitty to make another trip to Europe. The trip was partly in hope of finding a medical cure for Kitty's illness. While they did not speak about it much, it was obvious to Milton that his wife's health was declining. Kitty fell more often, and sometimes she had to use two canes to get around. On really bad days, Kitty was not able to get out of bed.

The doctors in Europe were not able to offer hope for Kitty. Despite ongoing medical breakthroughs, the prognosis that Dr. Erb had given Milton and Kitty in Germany eight years before remained the same. Milton was disappointed. He had hoped that by now there might have been some medical breakthrough.

While they were in Europe, Milton and Kitty had plenty of time to talk about their future. In the ten years since their wedding, they had accomplished much. But now Milton was fifty-one years old and Kitty was thirty-seven, and they had to face the fact that they would be childless for the rest of their lives, something that made them both sad. Without an heir, Milton was concerned about what would happen to his rapidly growing fortune. "It's a sin for a man to die rich," he told Kitty one day as they sat in their hotel room. "Besides, I can't see what happiness a rich man gets from continually acquiring things and not giving any of it away. After all, what's the point of money unless you use it for the good of the community and humanity in general?"

"I agree," Kitty replied. "Milton, I've been thinking that we should put our money into helping orphaned children. What do you think? We could start an orphanage and school for children right in Hershey." Kitty's eyes shined as she spoke. "We could convert the homestead into an orphanage. It would be a perfect place for children to run around."

Before he replied, Milton thought about the many times he had imagined himself living in the homestead surrounded by a happy, secure family. "I believe you're right, Kitty. The old place would make a wonderful home for orphaned children. In particular, I think I'd like to give unfortunate boys a chance at a good life. I hear that many orphan boys end up in jail because they have no one to guide them and teach them the skills they need to work hard and make the right decisions in life. If we do it, we'll have to find just the right house parents."

By the time Milton and Kitty returned to Pennsylvania in the fall of 1909, they had mapped out a plan for the Hershey Industrial School, as they were calling it. The new school was to be based on a "home farm" model. Initially about eight boys would be assigned to the farm, with a married couple to oversee their daily lives.

On November 15, 1909, Milton and Kitty signed their names to the new school's deed of trust. This document transferred 486 acres of land around the homestead as well as the existing buildings to the Hershey Trust Company to be used as an orphanage and school. The orphans, defined as boys whose fathers had died, were to be between the ages of four and eight. For a boy to be accepted into the new school, his guardian or a caregiver had to apply to the Hershey Industrial School Board of Managers, of which Milton served as chairman. The trust deed stated:

> All orphans admitted to the school shall be fed with plain, wholesome food; plainly, neatly, and comfortably clothed, without distinctive dress; and fittingly lodged. Due regard shall be paid to their health; their physical training shall be attended to, and they shall have suitable and proper exercise and recreation. They shall be instructed in the several branches of a sound education, agriculture, horticulture [and] gardening . . . bearing in mind that the main object in view is to train young men to useful trades and occupations, so that they can earn their own livelihood.

One other aspect of the boys' upbringing concerned Milton greatly—the boys' Christian values. Milton knew that instilling Christian values into the boys would depend in large part on choosing just the right house parents to run the school.

Milton's search to find the right couple to run the orphanage and school did not take him far from home. George Copenhaver had been hired to oversee the dairy farms that provided milk for the chocolate factory. When he heard about the school, he asked Milton to consider him and his wife for the job. Milton soon realized that George and Prudence Copenhaver were just the couple he was looking for. George was a calm, likeable young man, and both he and Prudence had been schoolteachers. They were both graduates of Berrysburg Lutheran Seminary and believed that Bible study and prayer should be an important part of each boy's daily life.

It took nearly a year to gather everything that was needed to get the new orphanage and school off to a good start. The Hershey homestead was out-fitted with beds and bathrooms, blackboards, and books. Milton and Kitty were involved in every step of the process. In August 1910 Milton interviewed a woman named Mrs. Wagner, who explained that her husband, a factory worker, had died, leaving her with six children. She took in washing and ironing to earn enough for her family to survive, but no mat-ter how hard she tried, she could not make enough money to support seven people. Milton and the school board accepted two of her sons, six-year-old Nelson and four-year-old Irvin, as the first two boys in the school. Jacob and Guy Weber quickly followed. Their father had been a pastor, and when he died, the only work their mother was able find was in a shirt factory. She worked long hours, which meant that there was no one to watch over her boys. She explained to Milton and the members of the school board that it was a difficult choice to make, but she had come to the conclusion that the best hope for her boys was to place them in the orphanage.

Now there were four boys to feed, clothe, and educate, and things got off to a good start. Although the boys were sad to be away from their mothers, they soon thrived, eating nutritious food and learn-ing their lessons. The school's early grades were modeled on the ideas of Friedrich Froebel, founder of the kindergarten movement, and emphasized learning through play and physical activity.

Several other boys were later accepted into the school, and each boy was expected to do chores in the homestead, out in the barn, and in the yard. When spring arrived, Prudence's brother came to the homestead to supervise the school garden. The boys helped to plant and weed their own crops. The fruit and vegetables they grew in the garden would be eaten throughout the rest of the year.

The Hershey Industrial School provided a good life for the boys, and Milton and Kitty were pleased to see them happy and cared for. Because of her progressing illness, Kitty seldom left the house. Milton made it a point to visit the boys at the school each Sunday to check up on them and enjoy their company. Fanny often accompanied her son on these Sunday visits. The boys particularly welcomed her, as she always carried with her a basket filled with Hershey chocolates to distribute.

Chapter 14

"I Think She's Gone"

It was Saturday, May 31, 1913, and people pressed together shoulder to shoulder along the parade route. American flags and red, white, and blue bunting hung from buildings and lampposts. A brass band led the way, and music from their instruments filled the air as they marched. Following the band were forty-five floats decorated with flowers and more bunting and flags. One of the floats carried Bob, a trained black bear that did tricks and waved to the crowd, and his trainer. Children cheered and pressed to get to the front for a closer look at the huge creature. Following the floats came another band and then marchers dressed in white, all moving together in close formation. Milton enjoyed every moment of the parade, the culmination of two days of celebration to mark the tenth anniversary of the founding of

Hershey, Pennsylvania. To Milton it seemed like only yesterday that the plan for the town had been laid and houses and other buildings had begun to rise in the pastureland around Derry Church.

The town of Hershey had become popular. It continued to grow as the need for more workers at the chocolate factory increased. Milton had added amenities for the residents of the town to use: a carousel, a swimming pool in the park, and the largest free private zoo in the United States. Along with Bob the bear, the zoo had deer, monkeys, lions, native possums, birds, and many other exotic and interesting animals. On weekends during the summer, thousands of people would flock to Hershey by train to picnic in the park, swim, ride the carousel, visit the zoo, and enjoy concerts at the open-air theater.

When Milton built the park, Fanny Hershey had chastised her son for doing so. As far as she was concerned, a park was a frivolous thing. However, over the years, Milton noted that his mother, clad in her plain clothing with a Mennonite bonnet on her head, was spending more and more time in the park. Fanny enjoyed watching the children as they rode the carousel and listening to concerts at the open-air theater.

Fanny was now seventy-eight years old and still as strong and helpful as ever. On Sundays she would walk around the chocolate factory, checking to make sure that all the doors were locked tight. Each day she insisted that a large box of Hershey Kisses be delivered to the house for her to wrap during the afternoon. Since this kept his mother content and feeling useful, Milton did not bother to tell her that the company could not sell the kisses she wrapped, as they had not been wrapped in an inspected facility.

While the town of Hershey began to thrive, so, too, did the Hershey Chocolate Company. Net sales had now reached five million dollars a year, and with the population of the United States growing rapidly, the market for Hershey chocolate seemed inexhaustible.

It had been three years since the first four boys had arrived at the Hershey Industrial School, and now the number of boys enrolled in the orphanage and school had swelled to thirty-five. The old experimental creamery and chocolate factory behind the homestead, where Milton had labored to unlock the secret of making milk chocolate, had been turned into a woodworking shop, and the boys loved it. They made desks, chairs, and bookshelves for the school. A separate outbuilding at the homestead was taken over for the kindergarten boys. Milton and Kitty had begun a tradition of hosting each class at the school for breakfast once a year. At these breakfasts they would give the boys presents and then quiz them on their schoolwork and leisure activities. Milton loved it when he heard that the boys were making kites to fly or exploring Spring Creek. He made trips to New York and Philadelphia to consult with education specialists to make sure that his school was doing the very best job it could possibly do to bring education, stability, and happiness to the orphan boys the school took in.

As far as Milton was concerned, everything was going well, except for one thing—Kitty was slowly dying, and they both knew it. Milton tried to make his wife's life as comfortable as possible. He brought her flowers every morning and showered her with gifts, and whenever possible he accompanied Kitty on trips to health spas or the seaside.

In January 1915, while Kitty was having a massage in her hotel room, Milton and his cousin Clayton Snavely walked along the boardwalk in Atlantic City, New Jersey. Milton stopped in front of a large Wrigley chewing-gum poster. "Clayton," Milton said. "I'm worried about Wrigley's enterprise. This new chewing-gum fad has become popular, and I hear that Bill Wrigley is now determined to go into the chocolate business and put me out of business."

"That would take a lot of doing," Clayton replied.

"Yes, I know. To think he can even imagine the possibility. But something has to be done. They're on a roll at the moment, and I'm thinking of fighting fire with fire." Clayton looked confused, and Milton continued. "I'm going into the chewing-gum business myself. What do you think of that?"

A week later Milton was back in Hershey and still thinking about selling chewing gum. He had spoken to Bill Murrie, now president of the company, about going into the gum business. Oddly enough, Bill knew of a chewing-gum manufacturer in New York who was going out of business and selling his equipment. Milton had an idea. He would send Clayton to New York to buy the equipment and learn everything he could about manufacturing chewing gum.

"Buy the equipment in your own name, Clayton, and don't say anything about your relationship to me. I want you to find out where to buy chicle, and at the best price. Take lots of notes. We're going to beat Bill Wrigley at his own game. Come back and tell me everything you can," Milton instructed his cousin.

Milton waited eagerly, and when Clayton returned, he had a rough idea of the recipe for making chewing gum and, most important, drums of chicle, the sticky sap of a tropical evergreen tree from Mexico and Central America that formed the basis of chewing gum. He also had with him five hundred dollars' worth of equipment: a mixer and attachments, a set of rolls and attachments, a chicle chopper, two scoring machines, thirty-six five-foot-long drying boards, twenty-four small drying boards, thirty-six chicle dryers, and a marble slab.

Once again Milton was in his element working out a new product to sell. He began experimenting with the recipe for chewing gum immediately, but his experimenting was soon interrupted by tragedy.

Kitty and her nurse, Ruth Beddoe, had made a short visit to Atlantic City. Even in the dreary winter months, Kitty found that the sea air helped her breathe better, and she enjoyed walking or being wheeled along the boardwalk. Milton was glad she had gone, but he was looking forward to his wife's return. On March 25, 1915, as he busied himself experimenting with chewing gum, Milton received a phone call around lunchtime from Ruth to say that she and Kitty had been forced to stop and spend the night at the Bellevue-Stratford Hotel in Philadelphia because of Kitty's constant coughing. Milton asked the nurse to call a local doctor to attend to his wife while he called for his chauffeur and raced off to join Kitty in Philadelphia.

By the time Milton arrived at the Bellevue-Stratford Hotel, the doctor had visited Kitty. Ruth met Milton in the lobby to tell him the doctor's diagnosis: Kitty was suffering from a severe attack of bronchitis, which, on top of her other illness, had made her very weak. The doctor believed that she would recover as long as she stayed tucked in a warm bed until the danger passed.

On hearing Ruth's report, Milton called the chocolate factory to let people there know he would not be returning immediately. He then headed upstairs to be with his wife. Kitty smiled as he entered the room. "Is there anything I can get for you?" he asked.

Kitty looked up mischievously. "A glass of champagne," she replied.

Milton smiled. "If that's what you want," he said as he turned to go back down to the lobby.

He had just reached the bottom of the stairs when Ruth called to him. "Mr. Hershey, you had better come quickly. Mrs. Hershey has changed her appearance."

Milton turned and bounded back up the stairs. When he reached the top, Ruth said quietly, "I'm sorry. I think she's gone."

Milton rushed to Kitty's side, lifted her hand, and felt for a pulse. There was none. He tried to take in the information. Was his forty-four-year-old wife really dead? Here in a hotel room in Philadelphia?

For the next twenty-four hours Milton was beside himself. He hardly remembered any of it, just that Kitty was dead and he was alone.

Milton was still in a daze as an assistant helped him plan the funeral. He decided to hold the funeral mass at the Cathedral of Saints Peter and Paul in Philadelphia, not too far from where he had opened his first candy business in the city in 1876. For the day of the funeral he closed down the chocolate factory in Hershey and paid the train fare of anyone who wanted to come to Philadelphia to attend the service. Twenty-seven limousines were hired to carry the mourners from the train station to the cathedral and back again after the service. For most of the service Milton wept openly, still trying to take in what had happened. Afterward he had Kitty's body placed in a vault in Philadelphia until a cemetery was established at Hershey. A cemetery was the one thing Milton had omitted to plan for in his "happy" town. Now he needed one.

For Milton, life without Kitty felt bleak and empty. He still had his chocolate factory and his plans to make chewing gum, but it all meant very little compared to losing his wife. He found it hard to concentrate on anything and spent a lot of time locked in his bedroom staring at photographs of Kitty and feeling as though nothing else would ever matter to him again. He was grateful, though, for visits from his old friend Lebbie. He and Lebbie would sit and reminisce about the old days at Milton's first candy company in Philadelphia and about starting the caramel company in Lancaster. Milton had never forgotten the way Lebbie had helped him when nobody else would. As they talked, Milton's focus began to shift back toward his chocolate business. Before long he was finding solace in work as he continued his chewing-gum experiments. The experimenting paid off when Milton eventually came up with a recipe for making gum that worked well.

With the chewing-gum recipe in hand, Milton began searching for a name for the new product and finally settled on Easy Chew. Soon blue-and-white packets of Easy Chew were rolling off the production line. A hundred employees at the factory were kept busy working fifty-four hours a week, churning out the new product.

During this time the town of Hershey continued to develop. It now had a new, state-of-the-art, four-thousand-seat convention hall, supplied with water from the town's newly installed filtered-water supply. The chocolate business kept on growing. By now annual sales were up to ten million dollars a year. To keep up with the national demand for Hershey products, the factory had grown to thirty-one buildings, and Milton now owned eighty-five hundred acres of dairy farmland around the area to help with the ever-increasing demand for milk for chocolate production.

Despite the rapid growth of his company, the thing that was the closest to Milton's heart was the orphanage and school where sixty orphan boys now proudly called themselves Milton's Boys. In fact, the school had outgrown the old Hershey homestead, and Milton implemented a new model. Groups of eight to ten boys, along with house parents, would live on one of his dairy farms. They would participate in the farm chores and attend school. Every Sunday Milton visited the various groups of boys, checking up on them and watching over their progress.

In early 1916, almost a year after Kitty's death, as a heavy blanket of snow lay on the ground, Milton decided it was time for a vacation. Normally he would have gone to Europe, but the region was mired in a bloody war, with Germany, the Austro-Hungarian Empire, and the Turkish Empire fighting against France, Great Britain, and their allies.

With a trip to Europe out of the question, Milton decided to go somewhere he had never been, somewhere warm and not too far away and where he would not be assailed with memories of Kitty. He knew just the place—the Caribbean island of Cuba. Milton had become interested in Cuba from reading about the exploits of Teddy Roosevelt and his Rough Riders during the Spanish-American War and subsequent capture of Cuba from Spain. Milton decided it was time to check out the country for himself. Not wanting to travel alone, he invited his mother and her companion, Leah Putt, to accompany him.

Milton set out from Hershey for Cuba, expecting to enjoy sunshine and the tropical setting. What he did not expect to do was to start a whole new venture in the Caribbean.

Chapter 15

Cuba

As the ship steamed into the harbor at Havana, Milton stood at the rail taking in the sights. A mass of buildings crowded together along the edge of Havana Bay. Even before the steamer docked, Milton could see that the streets of the city were alive with people. After disembarking ship, he was engulfed by a swirl of exotic colors, sounds, and smells. Milton loved the place from the start, though his mother and her friend Leah looked out of place. The Cubans quickly concluded that Fanny Hershey, dressed in her long black Mennonite dress with a matching black bonnet on her head, must be a Catholic nun from America. Milton chuckled every time he thought about his mother being mistaken for a nun.

Soon after arriving in Havana, Milton rented a small house for them all to stay in. His mother did not want to be put up in a hotel. She preferred to cook and clean for her son rather than watch other people do it for him. Once they were settled into the small house, Milton spent his time exploring Havana. The buildings were built in the neoclassical and Spanish colonial architectural styles. Milton was particularly impressed with the massive and beautiful Gran Teatro de la Habana (Great Theatre of Havana). How he wished Kitty were there with him to attend performances. Kitty had always loved the theater.

Milton also walked the Malecón, the broad esplanade and seawall that ran along the edge of the bay. Despite his mother's insistence that she cook for him, he managed to frequent several local restaurants and some of the city's many clubs and casinos.

Most of all Milton loved to hire a car and a driver and head out to explore the lush tropical countryside. After one of these long drives through the countryside, Milton described the trip to his mother, telling her about the miles and miles of shiny green sugarcane they had gone by. "Milton," his mother interrupted, "why don't you just buy a sugar plantation here in Cuba and set up a mill. You could help give the people good jobs and secure your sugar supply at the same time."

Milton looked up in astonishment. His mother never suggested he spend money on anything. She was always warning him to save it. But as he thought about her suggestion, he realized it was a sensible business move. Demand for Hershey products was reaching a new high. Nearly fifty boxcar loads of chocolate left the factory in Hershey every day except Sunday, and annual sales were now over ten million dollars a year. Since it was becoming more difficult to import refined sugar from Europe, Milton knew he could be in real trouble if sales kept increasing at the rate they were. He was concerned that the lingering war over there, along with rationing, might stop European sugar imports altogether. Already the price of sugar in the United States was climbing, and Milton knew that to stay competitive with the prices for his chocolate products he needed a steady supply of refined sugar.

The next day Milton hired a 1914 Model T Ford and a driver and asked to be driven to Matanzas, which lay on the coast about sixty miles east of Havana. The Model T chugged along, with the ocean on one side and sugarcane plantations on the other. Milton paid close attention to the men in the cane fields as they cut down the tall sugarcane with machetes and loaded it onto carts. The driver explained that the cut sugarcane would be taken to a local processing plant, where it would be squeezed and ground down to release the syrup from the cane. This syrup would then be evaporated to produce raw sugar.

The road was potholed in places, but when they reached Santa Cruz del Norte, about halfway to Matanzas, it became impassable for the Model T. The driver then arranged for a *volante*, a two-wheel, two-seater horse-drawn carriage used in Cuba. The body of the volante hung in front of the large unsprung wheels. To make up for the lack of springs, the seat was slung on pieces of leather that allowed it to move freely from the jolting body of the wagon. Unlike in the United States, the driver of this contraption sat astride one of the two horses that pulled it.

From Santa Cruz del Norte, Milton headed inland up the Yumirí Valley, a lush region set between two low mountains and populated by small farms. The ride in the volante was bumpy. Milton grumbled to himself that even though he was now twenty miles from the sea, for the first time in his life he felt seasick as the carriage seat swung back and forth. Milton's discomfort was rewarded when they climbed onto a plateau that overlooked the valley. Sugarcane grew on the plateau, and a refreshing breeze blew in off the sea. A spring fed a crystal clear stream, much like the spring that fed Spring Creek back in the Lebanon Valley. As Milton explored the land, a vision entered his head of a second Hershey town, just like the one in Pennsylvania, only in a tropical setting and with a factory that produced refined sugar, not chocolate. As he headed back down the Yumirí Valley, Milton wondered whether such a thing could be done. Could he get all the permits and equipment he would need to build a town in Cuba?

By the time he returned to Havana, Milton had made up his mind. He was going to buy sixty-five hundred acres of the sugarcane fields on the beautiful plateau and build a sugar refinery and town. The odds against success seemed insurmountable, but at fifty-nine years of age Milton decided that this was the invigorating challenge he needed at this point in his life. He would bring his old friend, civil engineer Henry Herr, to Cuba from Lancaster to do what he had done for Milton in Pennsylvania—survey the site and lay out a town and a factory. He also planned for an electric railway that would run all the way from Matanzas, through Milton's new town to Havana. Milton calculated that such a railway would be about sixty miles long and would be the only electric railroad in the country.

Best of all, Milton would provide a wonderful standard of living for his workers in the factory and town. Each house would have running water and electricity, something only the wealthiest Cubans enjoyed. Milton planned to build 180 houses, as well as dormitories for the single men. Although thousands of workers would be needed, he planned to offer cheap train tickets so that employees who lived farther away could commute to the refinery each day. He would also build a school, a library, and a general store and bring in doctors and nurses to keep everyone healthy.

While in Havana in April, Milton met Henry Ford, a man who had long been an inspiration to him. The two men enjoyed each other's company and soon became friends. Milton noted that the two of them took a similar approach to manufacturing: mass-producing their respective products in modern factories as cheaply as possible. They also were constantly searching for ways to streamline their manufacturing processes and so further cut production costs, giving them an edge over their competitors by being able to sell less-expensive products. That was what Milton was trying to do in building another town and sugar refinery in Cuba. He wanted to secure a stable supply of sugar for his chocolate company at a lower price than what his competitors could buy it for.

One day Henry Ford and Milton went sailing in Henry's boat, the *Sialia*, eastward along the north coast of Cuba toward Matanzas. As they sailed, they stopped at Santa Cruz del Norte, where Milton showed Henry Ford the land he intended to buy and explained to him what he planned to build there. As Milton laid out his plans, Henry listened closely, congratulating Milton on his farsightedness.

As Milton thought about the wonderful time he spent with Henry, his only regret was that his father had not lived long enough to meet the man. He was sure that the two of them would have gotten along very well. The two Henrys would, no doubt, have inspired each other to try new experiments.

Soon after his meeting with Henry Ford, Milton returned to Pennsylvania. Before leaving, he hired an agent in Cuba to oversee the process of buying the land he wanted for his refinery and town. Milton was eager to secure the land and recruit the people he would need to make his vision a reality.

Early in May 1916, Milton received word that the land deal had gone through, and he began traveling back and forth between Cuba and Pennsylvania to move the project along. The war in Europe made finding the building materials for the town and refinery challenging but not impossible. Milton ordered an electric train for the new railway line that was being built, along with all the specialized equipment needed to extract and refine sugar from cane in the refinery.

By 1917 the "Great War," as the war in Europe was now being called, had spread offshore. The Germans were launching submarine attacks on any English or American ship crossing the Atlantic Ocean. As a result, sugar shipments from Europe came to a halt, making it more important than ever for Milton to get his sugar refinery in Cuba up and running as soon as possible. In the meantime, to assure a regular sugar supply, Milton bought a small existing refinery at Central San Juan Bautista, located not too far from the Yumiri Valley in Cuba. (*Central* was the word used in Cuba to refer to a town that had sprung up around a sugar refinery.)

In April 1917 the sinking of seven neutral American merchant ships incensed the American public so much that the United States entered the war in Europe against Germany. As the US army mobilized soldiers to send to the fighting, it looked for ways to feed the troops on the battlefield. The army needed a four-ounce chocolate bar loaded with extra calories and vitamins that could be used as an emergency provision for soldiers and sailors. The bar had to stay solid in warm temperatures, since melted chocolate would be useless to the soldiers and sailors. The Hershey Chocolate Company rose to the challenge and created a chocolate bar that met the army's specifications. Soon huge orders began to roll in for the bar, first for one million bars and then two million. Milton needed all the help he could get at the factory to produce that many chocolate bars in a hurry. He even called for volunteers to help wrap and box up the chocolate bars for shipping. Three hundred women turned up at the factory to get the job done.

On November 11, 1918, the Great War in Europe came to an end. Great Britain, France, and their allies, including the United States, had won. To celebrate the event, a huge parade marched down Chocolate Avenue in Hershey. Flags waved and banners were draped from windows and balconies as the chocolate factory marching band played "God Bless America." Milton, for one, was glad the fighting was over, and he hoped to never see another war. Not only was the Mennonite tradition he had grown up in opposed to war, but also many young men from Hershey had been sent off to fight in Europe. A number had never returned, having been killed in the fighting.

The end of the war made Milton think about his enormous wealth: annual sales were now at twenty million dollars, and most of Milton's personal wealth was in Hershey Chocolate Company stock worth sixty million dollars. Milton was well aware that other multimillionaires were spending their fortunes on enormous homes and lavish yachts, things that did not appeal to him. At heart, he was still a Mennonite farm boy from Pennsylvania.

More than anything, Milton wanted to be remembered for building his orphanage and school and giving young boys the chance to grow up in the countryside, to feel secure and loved, and to make something of themselves. So quietly, two days after the end of the war, and without telling anyone but his lawyer, Milton did something extraordinary. He signed over his sixty million dollars' worth of company stock to the Hershey Industrial School. The money was to be held in trust and used to fund the operation of the orphanage and school so that orphans for generations to come would have a place to call home. This gift represented about 90 percent of Milton's wealth, and he went to bed that night a happy man. It had been nearly three and a half years since Kitty died, and that day Milton knew he had done something for both of them, something his wife would have been very proud of.

Despite challenges, the Cuban enterprise continued to grow on time, and in January 1919 the new Hershey sugar refinery began processing its first crop of sugar cane. Workers at the refinery moved into houses at the new town, which was called Central Hershey, and as the new electric train began running, a spirit of optimism filled the air.

With the Cuba sugar operation under way, Milton decided to visit Europe once again. He was in Paris in October 1919 and found it odd to be there alone. On past visits he'd had Kitty with him, and they had attended the theater together and visited art galleries and dined at fine restaurants. From Paris he traveled to Marseille on the south coast of France in November, and by Christmas he was in Monte Carlo. Milton was still in Monte Carlo in January when he received a telegram from Hershey saying that his eighty-four-year-old mother had pneumonia. Milton booked the first available passage on a ship back to the United States and was at his mother's bedside by mid-February.

Milton did everything he could to make his mother comfortable. Despite his best effort, Fanny did not recover and died on March 11, 1920. After the funeral Milton had his mother's body buried at the new Hershey cemetery, where Kitty's remains were now also buried. Not content until his family was together at last, Milton had his father's remains exhumed from the old family plot and placed in the new cemetery. Now when he went to visit the graves, he could see all three of their graves together in one place.

Following his mother's death, Milton felt very much alone. Everyone who had believed in him at the beginning—Aunt Mattie, his father, and now his mother—was gone. Milton was glad, however, that his mother had lived to see the chocolate business become such an amazing success. Sales had risen to fifty-eight million dollars the year before Fanny died. Sometimes, when Milton visited her grave, he would remember his mother's words and smile: "Be careful, Milton. Your money will go. It will all go sometime." In the summer of 1920, any chance of that happening seemed unlikely. Little did Milton know that the possibility was just months away.

Chapter 16

Futures

In early May 1920, Milton sat studying the graph in front of him that showed the cost of sugar every year since the beginning of the war. The line on the graph ascended steeply. Each year the cost of sugar was becoming a bigger part of the chocolate company's budget. By now Milton had acquired another sugar refinery in Cuba, located at Central Rosario. Although it and the other two refineries (Central Hershey and Central San Juan Bautista) produced thirty million pounds of sugar in 1920, it was not enough to keep up with the demand at the chocolate factory. The factory needed to buy more sugar, a lot more.

Milton drummed his fingers on the desk, trying to think through the smartest plan. If the price of sugar kept going up at the same rate, it could cost Milton hundreds of thousands of dollars more to buy sugar two years from now. But there was something he could do about the situation: he could lock in the price he would pay for sugar for the next two years at twenty-six cents per pound. It was a gamble, betting that the price of sugar would keep going up and that it was better to buy "futures" now instead of paying the full price later.

Milton thought long and hard about the risk of buying sugar futures. He decided to pay the twenty-six cents now and hope that the price of sugar would continue to climb so that other candy companies would have to pay the higher price, giving him a competitive edge. Now all Milton could do was wait and see whether his gamble would pay off.

Within a month the line on the graph had stopped its steep ascent, and by July it was headed downward. Milton watched helplessly as tons of sugar from refineries in Cuba were dumped onto the American market. Sugar prices fell fast. By January 1921 sugar was selling on the open market for four cents a pound. Milton felt sick. His futures contract meant that he was stuck buying the sugar he needed at twenty-six cents a pound.

When it was over, Milton's gamble on sugar futures had cost his chocolate company over two and a half million dollars. The Hershey Chocolate Company had gone from having a rosy six-million-dollar profit the year before to being in the red for the first time in its history.

To make matters worse, Milton's chewing-gum manufacturing was also a failure. When Milton began producing chewing gum, his competitors, such as the Wrigley Company, were putting five sticks of gum in a pack. William Murrie, president of the Hershey Chocolate Company, suggested they put six sticks in each pack of Easy Chew gum and sell it for the price of five. Milton liked the idea, and so packs of gum containing six sticks were produced.

The American public liked the idea of getting an extra stick of gum for the price of five, but the Wrigley Company did not. It took the matter up with the federal government, pointing out that the Hershey Chocolate Company was selling six sticks of gum per pack, but paying tax on only five sticks. At the urging of the Wrigley Company, the government put an additional tax on Milton's chewing gum. The decision angered Milton, who pointed out that he was being unfairly penalized, since he was giving the public an extra stick of gum at the same price that his competitors charged. However, the extra tax remained in place.

To make matters worse still, following the war, restrictions were put on the importation of raw materials for the manufacturing of products that were deemed to be nonessential. Unfortunately for Milton, chewing gum was not regarded as an essential product, and soon he found it difficult to get the extra sugar and chicle he needed to manufacture it. Milton tried to keep chewing-gum production going, but with the extra tax he was forced to pay and the difficulty of getting raw material, he decided to discontinue his line of chewing gum.

With two failures on his hands, Milton had to decide what to do next. In reality he had few choices, and he needed to borrow a large sum of money to keep his company afloat. He approached National City Bank, who agreed to give Milton a ten-million-dollar mortgage against the chocolate factory as long as he agreed to one thing—having a financial controller of the bank's choosing on his staff. This man would be in charge of the financial decisions the company made until the loan was paid back. Milton hated the thought of giving up that sort of control and having someone from New York shadowing his every move, poking into the company books, and asking endless questions. But he had little choice and so agreed to the bank's terms.

Soon R. J. DeCamp, National City Bank's appointed financial controller, was seated at a desk next to Milton. He turned out to be every bit as difficult to work with as Milton had imagined. R. J. expected to be treated like royalty, and when he visited Cuba to check on how well the sugar-refining business was doing, he booked himself into a very expensive hotel in Havana. Milton drew the line at that. He objected strenuously to spending money on an expensive hotel when there was a perfectly comfortable hacienda in which R. J. could stay at the sugar refinery in Central Rosario. Milton won the argument.

Milton knew the only way to get R. J. off his back was through hard work, and lots of it. He called together his top advisers, John Snyder and Bill Murrie, and explained the situation to them. The three of them agreed on a plan. They called a meeting of the managers at the chocolate factory and asked them to help turn the situation around. Milton made a personal plea to the group.

"It's not my personal wealth that matters here," Milton began. "That's not the goal. What's at stake is the future of the orphan boys and their school and the future of all the Hershey workers. Please do not consider me your ruler. I am a fellow citizen of this town, and Hershey belongs to all of us. It is *our* business, not *my* business. Join with me in doing everything you can to save that business. Work hard and tell your boss if you can see any way to save labor or materials. Don't sacrifice quality but find ways to get your jobs done as efficiently as possible. Let's roll up our sleeves and get to work."

Milton led by example. At sixty-five years of age he arrived at his office desk at seven o'clock each morning. He walked the factory floor, questioning workers about the most efficient way to get things done and urging the employees to work harder and smarter. Others soon caught his enthusiasm, and everyone began to pull together to pay off the bank loan and get the company back on track. The effort was successful. After suffering a four-hundred-thousand-dollar loss, the company was profitable again the following year.

As sales of Hershey chocolate kept growing, so did the profits, so much so that National City Bank decided its loan was safe and recalled R. J. back to New York. The bank returned full control of the company to Milton, who described it as one of the best days of his life. Once again he had shown that hard work and dedication could turn a situation around.

The crisis helped Milton realize that times had changed. The company, the orphanage and school, and the town were too big to be run by one person. Although he did not feel the need to slow down, Milton wanted to share the load with others. He divided the company into three parts: the Hershey Chocolate Corporation, which owned the chocolate properties and was the main generator of profit; Hershey Estates, which administered the town and all its various services; and the Hershey Corporation, which owned the sugar refineries in Cuba.

With the company now separated into three entities, Milton continued to divide his time between Pennsylvania and Cuba. He had the stately old hacienda at Central Rosario renovated, and he stayed there whenever he was in the country. Milton loved the Cuban people, and he considered it a privilege to be able to provide four thousand people with good jobs and nice homes. The Hershey employees in Cuba were treated well, unlike many of the employees of other big American companies.

On November 18, 1923, word leaked out that Milton Hershey had invested his entire fortune in helping orphan boys. The story made the front page of the *New York Times*, and reporters from various newspapers came to Hershey to write articles about the town, its founder, and its people. James Young, writing in the *Times*, called Hershey "the town of smiles." He reported that there were now three hundred orphan boys being taken care of at the Hershey Industrial School. In an interview for the newspaper, Milton explained why he had given 90 percent of his money to the orphan boys. "I am sixty-six years old and do not need much money," he said. "My business has been far more successful than I ever expected it to be. . . . I have no heirs—that is, no children. So I decided to make the orphan boys of the United States my heirs."

As for his hopes for the boys, Milton said, "We do not expect to turn out a race of college professors. We want to help the boys of the masses to become good American citizens—farmers, artisans, and some of them perhaps businessmen ultimately—leaders in the mercantile, industrial, and social life of their communities."

About the same time in 1923, a train wreck in Cuba inspired Milton to include Cuban boys in his vision for a better tomorrow. Two oncoming trains, both belonging to the Hershey Electric Railway, collided on a blind curve, killing thirty people. As a result of the wreck, several children were orphaned, and Milton decided to take responsibility for them. Work on a new orphanage and school at Central Rosario began immediately after the wreck, and in February 1925 the doors to the new facility were opened to the first group of boys. The aims of this second orphanage and school were similar to those of the first one in Hershey. The boys were given a nice home to live in, house parents, a sound education, and vocational training to prepare them for a job once they graduated. Milton was excited about the new orphanage and school and was as dedicated to its success as he was to the orphanage and school in Hershey, Pennsylvania.

As the 1920s rolled on, the United States pros-
pered, and so did the Hershey Chocolate Corporation.
Americans liked the Hershey brand and the flavor of
their chocolate and continued to buy Hershey bars
in record numbers. Milton's chocolate company also
benefited from the growing number of other candy
companies that had sprung up producing chocolate
confections, such as the Curtiss company of Chicago with its Baby Ruth bar; the Mars company, also
from Chicago, with the Milky Way bar; and the Reese
company and its Peanut Butter Cups. Almost all of
these other candy companies bought the chocolate
coating they used to cover their various bars and
confections from Milton, helping his company profits
grow each year. Milton couldn't have been happier.
After the financial mess he had gotten the chocolate
company into with sugar futures in the early 1920s,
it was good to see company bank accounts again
ballooning.

   In February 1929 Milton's eighty-four-year-
old friend Lebbie died. At Lebbie's funeral Milton
thought back to how kind the man had been to him
over the years. Lebbie had offered Milton a place to
stay when his family had grown weary of him. He
had helped financially when it seemed unlikely that
Milton would ever be a successful businessman.
Lebbie had been with Milton when he started his
first failed candy business in Philadelphia in 1876
and had lived to see the Hershey Chocolate Corporation become the most successful chocolate company in the United States. After the funeral Milton
commented to Bill Murrie, "I've just buried the best

friend I ever had." The last of the old guard from Milton's early ventures into the candy-making business was gone, and Lebbie would be deeply missed. Now there was no one left for Milton to reminisce with about those early years in the candy-making business.

By 1929 sales of Hershey chocolate had reached forty-one million dollars, and the Cuban refineries were now producing thirty-one million tons of sugar per year, more than Milton's factories needed. Milton sold the excess sugar to the Coca-Cola Company, creating a strong bond between the two companies and helping to increase Hershey's profits. The golden days of American enterprise were going strong, but clouds hung over what appeared to be a stable economy. No one, including Milton, could have predicted how drastically things would change in October 1929.

Chapter 17

Time for Bold Action

I fully expect things to get worse, much worse, before they get better," Milton declared as he gazed around the room at his four closest advisers. "But I don't want us to become fearful. Now is the time for bold action. I intend to start four new buildings in Hershey—a hotel, a junior/senior high school for the boys, new offices for the chocolate factory, and a sports arena. We'll tackle them in that order. And of course, we'll finish the community building that was started last year. No need to slow that down at all. The rest of the United States might be in a depression, but here in Hershey, we're going to be in the middle of the biggest building boom this town has seen since it was founded. I think it will cost about ten million dollars, but it will be the best ten million I've ever spent. What do you all think?"

Milton stopped talking and waited. The objections soon flowed: Shouldn't they hold on to their spare cash to tide them over if things got worse? What if they didn't have enough money to finish the project? Perhaps they should just start with one building. What if people stopped buying chocolate altogether—what would be the point of brand-new buildings then?

Milton smiled to himself as he listened to his friends. He understood how they felt, but deep in his heart he knew he was right. "The way through this depression is to throw every ounce of energy into moving forward, planning, building. Think of the jobs it will create. Right now we have six hundred construction workers in town who need work. If we don't give them something to do, I'll have to give them money to keep them from starving. I would rather pay a man to work than to sit idle. And think about when these buildings are completed. They will create more jobs. The hotel will need cooks and waiters and maids, the junior/senior high school will need teachers, and the sports arena will need cleaners and groundskeepers and hotdog vendors. This building boom will set Hershey up for years to come, you mark my words."

The four men sat silently. Milton took that as a good sign. "Can I count on your support then?" he asked. One by one the men mumbled yes.

"Oh, and one more thing. We need a country club and a golf course." Someone groaned and Milton laughed. "Don't worry, we'll have to work on the golf course, but the clubhouse is already built. I'm going to donate High Point to be the clubhouse for the country club. I'm seventy-three years old now. I don't need the whole place to myself. I'm just going to keep two rooms on the top floor to live in. That will be enough for me. And I've decided to give away a hundred memberships to the country club. You will get the first four."

This time the men smiled. "Perhaps moving forward is the best way to go. It certainly feels better than retrenching," one of them murmured. The others agreed.

Milton left the meeting with his advisers invigorated. There was so much to do! He called in architect D. Paul Witmer and described his vision for Hotel Hershey. He wanted the hotel to be situated atop Pat's Hill on the north side of town overlooking downtown Hershey, the park, and the chocolate factory. The architecture for the building was to be in the Spanish style, and the hotel would have 170 rooms, a round dining room, and a lobby with a fountain.

Soon plans for the hotel were drawn up, and construction began in October 1931. With the hotel under way, Milton turned his attention to the new junior/senior high school, situated on the side of Pat's Hill below the hotel. Plans for the new school included an eighty-foot-tall clock tower that would be visible from all over town.

While construction continued on the hotel and the foundation for the new school was being dug, the community building began to emerge in downtown Hershey. This six-story building was big enough to include two movie theaters, a dining room and cafeteria, an indoor swimming pool, gymnasium, bowling alley, boxing and fencing rooms, and a photography darkroom. Over eight hundred stone-masons, plumbers, electricians, carpenters, brick-layers, and laborers were kept busy working on the various building sites. Another three hundred work-ers labored at the Hershey lumberyard, building the necessary furniture that would be needed to furnish the new structures.

Meanwhile, outside of Hershey, the Great Depres-sion engulfed the country. By 1932 the unemploy-ment rate in the United States had soared to 25 percent. Food riots took place in the Midwest, and panhandlers were on every corner in New York City. Milton was proud that not one person in Hershey was hungry or jobless. The depression had also caused a surge in the number of boys applying to attend the Hershey Industrial School. Three hundred boys had been enrolled in the school in 1930. Two years later that number had swelled to five hundred boys, with hundreds more on the waiting list.

The depression also caused sales of Hershey prod-ucts to dip. In 1933 sales totaled twenty-two million dollars, about half of what they had been four years before. Still, while the chocolate company was selling fewer items, profits stayed about the same because the price of ingredients had fallen dramatically.

On May 26, 1933, Hotel Hershey was formally opened. Four hundred guests were treated to a lav-ish dinner at which Milton managed to give a short speech. He said, "I am a simple farmer. I like to utilize nature's beauty for the pleasure of men. This hotel where you are assembled has been a dream of mine for many years."

The hotel had cost two million dollars to build and had kept many people in work. As Milton showed his dinner guests around the new place, he felt sure that it would be a focal point for the town for years to come. In true fashion, he couldn't help but think how well a set of reflecting ponds and a rose garden would look nearby.

Soon after the opening of the hotel, Milton went to Cuba to check on his sugar refineries and orphanage and school. He was delighted to see that both his sugar refinery business and the school were doing well. While he was in Cuba, Milton was given one of the greatest honors of his life. Cuban president Gerardo Machado awarded him the order of Carlos Manuel de Céspedes for his "unstinting interest in the welfare of Cuba." It was the highest honor that Cuba could confer on a foreigner. As he presented the medal, President Machado said to Milton, "You have presented to the world a truly admirable organization on Cuban soil. . . . The order of Carlos Manuel de Céspedes has not been given out often. We concede it only when a bit of our soul and all of our admiration goes with it."

Back in Hershey, Pennsylvania, the community building was officially opened on Labor Day weekend of 1933 as the town celebrated the thirtieth anniversary of its founding. The six-story stone building with its tiled roof was an imposing structure in the center of town. In fact, the house in which Milton's mother had lived until her death had been torn down to make way for the wing of the building containing the two theaters. The place had the most up-to-date amenities, and Milton was proud of the structure and the services and facilities it offered the community. Henry Wallace, US Secretary of Agriculture, spoke at the dedication. Milton was also scheduled to make a speech at the dedication ceremony, but when it came time for him to speak, he was too shy to step up to the podium in front of the large crowd gathered for the event. "Let other people do the talking," he told his assistant. "I'll just get on with doing the work."

There was still much to do. With the hotel and community building now open and the junior/senior high school nearing completion, it was time to focus on the new office building at the factory and the sports arena.

Over the years the chocolate factory had grown. It was now a multistory facility spread over many acres of land along Chocolate Avenue, and a new office building for the operation was long overdue. Milton always loved trying something new, which is what he did with the new office building for the chocolate factory. The new building was completely windowless. Instead, outdoor scenes were painted onto the interior walls in place of windows, and the indoor environment was controlled by central air-conditioning along with "scientifically" planned artificial lighting. Glass partitions were used in place of internal walls. The exterior of the building was in the art-deco style and was built from local limestone.

In September 1934 construction of the new junior/senior high school for the Hershey Industrial School was completed. The school was an impressive structure perched on the side of Pat's Hill. It was 780 feet long and comprised thirteen interconnected buildings. Five of these buildings contained classrooms, while the other eight were workshops where boys could learn metal and woodworking crafts as well as ceramics and mechanics. It also had a gymnasium that could seat three thousand people. By now 650 boys were enrolled in the Hershey Industrial School, and more boys arrived every week.

A year later the new office building was completed, and workers moved into it. In truth, the building got mixed reviews from those who worked in it. Some liked the controlled interior environment, with its light system in each office to indicate the weather outside: white for clear sky, red for rain, and green for snow. Other workers, though, pined for real windows, not painted scenes on the wall, so they could see what was going on outside.

With construction of the new office building complete, Milton turned his focus on the new sports arena. The arena was to seat seven thousand people for hockey games and ten thousand for concerts. With this building Milton again favored a new, experimental approach. The sports arena would be composed of a barrel vault roof made of concrete three and a half inches thick, stiffened and strengthened with steel ribs. Because of the unique barrel vault design, the roof would support its own weight without interior support columns, giving the spectators an unobstructed view. The crown of the roof would be one hundred feet above the floor. No building had ever been built this way in the United States, and it presented many interesting challenges. The engineers and builders on the site overcame them, and the new sports arena opened on December 19, 1936. Milton wished his father were there to see the new arena. Henry would have loved the modern approach to its construction.

Although all the building and development in Hershey had managed to stave off many of the effects of the Great Depression on the community, the previous seven years of economic hardship had left many workers in the United States demanding better working conditions and wages. Workers began forming themselves into unions that gave them the power to stand up against their employers. Milton, closely focused on keeping Hershey growing, hardly noticed as these new unions flexed their muscles in various parts of the country.

Strikes were held against low wages and poor working conditions at such companies as Berkshire Knitting Mills; the Firestone tire plant in Akron, Ohio; Bendix Products in South Bend, Indiana; RCA; General Motors, Ford, and Chrysler; and even the *Seattle Post-Intelligencer* newspaper. The list went on and on. Many of these were sit-down strikes, which meant workers sat down at their jobs, refusing to leave the factory so that others could not be hired to take their place. Tensions ran high, and strike events often erupted into violence. On May 30, 1937, Memorial Day, Chicago police opened fire on a parade of striking steelworkers and their families at the gate of the Republic Steel Company. Fifty people were shot, ten of whom died, while one hundred others were brutally beaten with clubs.

Despite these events, Milton was shocked when one of his plant managers burst into his room at High Point on April 2, 1937. "It's a strike, Mr. Hershey. The workers have shut down the electricity to the plant and are sitting down."

Milton was both bewildered and furious. "What do they want? They get good wages and wonderful working conditions. Hershey is the best place in the country to live. It has schools for the children, parks, and concerts. I don't understand. We haven't laid off a single employee during the depression. Why a strike here? What do they want?"

Milton soon learned that the strike involved approximately five hundred to six hundred workers of the more than three thousand workers employed at the chocolate factory. This minority of workers, however, had taken over the factory and barricaded themselves inside. Over the next several days, Milton and his executives met with the strike leaders, who were part of a union that the Congress of Industrial Organizations (CIO) had organized a month before. The strike leaders' biggest demand was that their union represent all the workers at the chocolate factory and that management collect union dues from each worker. Deeply disturbed by the strike, Milton left the negotiating to his lawyers and company executives.

Many of those who worked at the chocolate factory did not support the strike, but they could not go to work, because the factory had closed down.

Many others living in and around Hershey did not work directly for the factory, but their livelihoods were affected by the strike. Of these, dairy farmers suffered the greatest impact. With the factory closed down, the fresh milk the farmers shipped to the creamery each day to be processed into skim milk for the chocolate-making process sat in tanks on the farms, turning sour until it had to be dumped. And dumping the milk was costing the farmers money. As the strike entered its second and then third day, the farmers found their frustration boiling over, and they decided to take matters into their own hands.

On Tuesday, April 6, 1937, a march was organized through Hershey to show support for the company and to protest against the strikers. Eight thousand people, including dairy farmers and citizens of Hershey, marched that day, looping their route past High Point to make sure Milton knew he had their support.

The following morning the frustrated dairy farmers and the factory workers issued an ultimatum to the strikers: they were to leave the factory by noon or face the consequences. When 1:00 p.m. came and went and the strikers had made no attempt to evacuate the factory, the crowd decided to act. Brandishing clubs, axe handles, baseball bats, pipes, and even pitchforks, they attacked, bursting into the factory and catching the strikers off guard. When it was all over, the strike had been broken, but many of the strikers were badly beaten and needed to be hospitalized, and several of them had suffered stab wounds from pitchforks.

During the battle with the strikers, Milton stayed at High Point. His friends and managers gathered around to bring him news and discuss what to do next. Milton wept when he learned that several of "his boys" from the school had been hurt in the fighting, but he was relieved that the strike had finally ended.

With the strike over, the factory was quickly cleaned up, and workers were soon back doing what they and the company did best—making chocolate. However, Milton had to accept that times had changed. In the end he had to allow unions into the factory, and the connection he felt to his workers was never quite the same. He no longer walked the factory floor, encouraging the workers as he once had.

Chapter 18

Simple, Long-Ago Days

For he's a jolly good fellow. For he's a jolly good fellow. For he's a jolly good fel-low, and so say all of us!"

Milton stumbled backward a little as he entered the new arena, which was not yet even a year old, and heard eight thousand voices singing loudly. The crowd quickly followed this by launching into a rousing version of "Happy Birthday."

It was the evening of September 13, 1937, Milton Hershey's eightieth birthday. Milton had expected to celebrate the occasion quietly, especially after the recent union problems at the factory, but it appeared the people of Hershey had other ideas. Soon Milton was seated on a platform. In the center of the hockey rink sat a huge birthday cake, twelve feet across and holding eighty burning candles. Surrounding the cake was the Community Theatre orchestra and boys from the Hershey Industrial School, all standing tall in their brown and gold uniforms.

The crowd cheered as Milton stood to address them, but try as he may, he could not get words to flow from his mouth. Milton looked around the arena at all the people—workers, mothers, children, and supervisors. Some he'd known for thirty years or more, while others were relatively new citizens to the town. As Milton looked around, his eyes filled with tears. "These are my people," Milton murmured before sitting down. The crowd again cheered, and Milton's employees then presented him with a gift of a gold ring engraved with the earliest Hershey chocolate logo surrounded by eighteen diamonds. Cake and ice cream were served to everyone.

That night Milton went home a happy man, but he awoke to a nightmare. During the night, he had suffered a stroke and could now hardly move. Dr. Herman Hostetter, Milton's personal physician, rushed to his side. As the doctor examined his patient, he shook his head. The prognosis was not good. Dr. Hostetter announced that he did not expect Milton to live more than a week, or a month at the most.

For days Milton lay in bed, his life hanging by a thread, but he did not die. Slowly, very slowly, he began to recover. He started to eat again and then to talk a little. Amazingly, by Christmas Milton was back at the chocolate factory experimenting with new concoctions, many of them an attempt to add various foods with lots of vitamins into the chocolate. Milton ground and dehydrated celery, beets, turnips, and parsley and stirred them into chocolate, hoping to make an extra-nutritious Hershey bar. But none of the vegetable-laced chocolate passed the taste test, though the beet chocolate was pronounced edible. Undeterred, Milton continued experimenting with carrots, raisins, and cornmeal to make a nutritious bar. But none of the bars made it to market.

While Milton was busy with his experiments, something else was being developed at the factory. In April 1937 the US military asked the Hershey Chocolate Corporation to come up with a new, improved chocolate bar that could be use for everyday rations in a soldier's emergency kit. The six-hundred-calorie bar needed to stay fresh and solid in freezing temperatures as well as those of the tropics. It had to be sealed in packaging in such a way that it could be submerged in water for an hour and remain dry. Bill Murrie and the company's head chemist, Sam Hinkle, got to work on the project, which Milton took a keen interest in.

Sam determined that the ingredients for the new ration bar would be chocolate liquor, sugar, skim milk powder, cocoa butter, oat flour, vanillin, and thiamine hydrochloride as a source of Vitamin B1. When these ingredients were mixed together, they created a heavy paste that had to be pressed into molds to set rather than poured like normal chocolate. The men eventually came up with a ration bar that the military was happy with.

Producing the bar in the factory proved challenging. Because the normal chocolate-production process was based on the chocolate's being liquid until it was poured into molds and set, it followed easily from one step of the production process to the next. Not so with the thick paste of the new ration bar. As a result, special machinery and new processing systems had to be developed for the bar.

In September 1939 war broke out again in Europe, with Great Britain, France, and their allies fighting the Germans. The British were also fighting the Japanese in Southeast Asia as Japan tried to take over much of the region and establish an empire. None of this mattered much in the United States until December 7, 1941, when Japanese aircraft bombed Pearl Harbor in Hawaii. This led to the United States entering the war, which was now being fought on a global scale. Milton was sad to see the country embroiled in another war. He remembered the First World War and the horrific toll it had inflicted on the young men who had gone off to fight for the United States. Now it was about to happen again. Milton feared that many boys from the industrial school and the town would soon be drafted into the military and sent overseas to fight.

Orders for Field Ration D, as the newly developed chocolate bar was named, were in high demand. Through the course of the war, the military ordered one billion ration bars from the Hershey Chocolate Corporation. The company had five Army-Navy "E" awards bestowed upon it for its efforts in making the Field Ration D bar. The Army Air Force even named a B-26 bomber *The City of Hershey*.

Milton was proud of these awards and the role his company was playing in provisioning the men of the US military, yet he longed for the day when the war would be over. So many of "his boys" from the school were fighting overseas, and he frequently received a telegram informing him of one of their deaths. By the time the war ended on September 2, 1945, thirty-eight of his boys had died in the fighting.

To mark the end of the war and to remember those who had given their lives in both the First and Second World Wars, Milton proposed a new venture. This time it was not a building but a large athletic field for all nineteen hundred of the public school children who lived in Hershey. Memorial Field, as he named the complex, would cover thirty-six acres of land that he would donate to the project. It would include basketball courts, a baseball diamond, football fields, and a bowling green. It was just the kind of project Milton now enjoyed. Others would do most of the planning, while Milton was able to help design the fields and imagine the fun the children would have playing on them.

By now Milton did not go to the factory often. He had slowed down a lot over the past few years, and usually one or two nurses accompanied him everywhere he went. A lot of the time these nurses acted more like companions than medical staff, playing chess with him and reading his favorite novels to him in the evenings.

As Milton's eighty-eighth birthday approached on September 13, 1945, he wanted to do something special to mark the event, though not on the huge scale of his eightieth birthday party. He decided to have a special meal prepared for him and fourteen of his longtime colleagues. Someone suggested that rather than have the meal at the country club, they meet at the old Hershey homestead and dine in the room where Milton and his father were both born. Milton agreed, and the head chef at Hotel Hershey prepared a delicious meal for them all.

It was a somber meal for the men. In the corner of the room in which they ate at the homestead stood an old wood-turned cradle that Milton's mother had rocked him in as a baby eighty-eight years before. Milton did not say much, and his eyes grew teary as he listened to each man give a toast. He also thought about all that this room meant to him. He had been born in the house and returned there from Oil City when he was four years old.

Milton's memories of those early days when his parents had returned to Derry Church were vivid: breathing the fresh air, collecting eggs, and going to the market with his mother. Those days were simple, long-ago days, and the world was now a very different place. People traveled in fast cars and by airplane, listened to radios, and talked to each other on the telephone. But there was something that Milton hoped had stayed the same—the wonder of a small boy feeling safe and loved and at home in the beautiful Pennsylvania countryside. Milton hoped that all the boys in his industrial school felt that simple connection to others and to nature, and the simple pleasure of looking after animals and tending the land.

Exactly one month after his eighty-eighth birthday celebration, on October 13, 1945, Milton Snavely

Hershey died. His death came quickly. He had come down with pneumonia on October 11 and was admitted to the hospital. Two days later his heart stopped beating.

News of Milton's death spread, and the town went into mourning for its founder and benefactor. Every business and school in Hershey closed in Milton's honor. His body lay in state in the foyer of the junior/senior high school for three days. In that time thousands of people filed past the casket. Condolences flowed into Hershey from around the world, and hundreds of bouquets of flowers were delivered until they were several feet deep and spilling outside onto the steps. Milton's funeral was held at the high school, and twelve hundred people attended it. Eight young men, selected from among the 657 students of the Hershey Industrial School, served as pallbearers. After the service, two hundred cars lined up to escort Milton's body to its final resting place beside Kitty and Milton's parents. The four graves lay side by side, with a large, curved monument bearing the name "Hershey" encompassing them all.

Each year on November 15, the children of the school—Milton and Kitty's children—lay wreathes on the couple's graves. The anniversary marks the signing of the deed of trust that established the Hershey Industrial School (since renamed the Milton Hershey School) and provided the school with funds in perpetuity.

Bibliography

Brenner, Joël Glenn. *The Emperors of Chocolate: Inside the Secret World of Hershey and Mars.* New York: Random House, 2000.

Castner, Charles Schuyler. *One of a Kind: Milton Snavely Hershey, 1857–1945.* Hershey, Pa.: The Derry Literary Guild, 1983.

D'Antonio, Michael. *Hershey: Milton S. Hershey's Extraordinary Life of Wealth, Empire, and Utopian Dreams.* New York: Simon & Schuster, 2006.

McMahon, James D., Jr. *Milton Hershey School.* Charleston, S.C.: Arcadia Publishing, 2007.

Shippen, Katherine B., and Paul A. W. Wallace. *Milton S. Hershey.* New York: Random House, 1959.

About the Authors

Janet and Geoff Benge are a husband and wife writing team with more than twenty years of writing experience. Janet is a former elementary school teacher. Geoff holds a degree in history. Together they have a passion to make history come alive for a new generation of readers.

Originally from New Zealand, the Benges make their home in the Orlando, Florida, area.